Deathbed Wisdom
of the
Hasidic Masters

The Book of Departure
and Caring for People
at the End of Life

Translation and Annotation by
Rabbi Joel H Baron and Rabbi Sara Paasche-Orlow
Foreword by Arthur Green

For People of All Faiths, All Backgrounds
JEWISH LIGHTS Publishing
Woodstock, Vermont

Deathbed Wisdom of the Hasidic Masters:
The Book of Departure *and Caring for People at the End of Life*

2016 Quality Paperback Edition, First Printing
© 2016 by Joel H Baron and Sara Paasche-Orlow
Foreword © 2016 by Arthur Green

For information regarding permission to reprint material from this book, please write or fax your request to Jewish Lights Publishing, Permissions Department, at the address / fax number listed below, or email your request to permissions@ jewishlights.com.

Library of Congress Cataloging-in-Publication Data
Names: Mintz, Binyamin, author. I Baron, Joel H., 1943– translator, writer of added commentary. I Paasche-Orlow, Sara, 1967– translator, writer of added commentary. I Mintz, Binyamin. Sefer ha-histalkut. English.
Title: Deathbed wisdom of the Hasidic masters : the Book of departure and caring for people at the end of life / translation and annotation by Rabbi Joel H. Baron and Rabbi Sara Paasche-Orlow ; foreword by Arthur Green.
Description: Woodstock, VT : Jewish Lights Publishing, a division of LongHill Partners, Inc., [2016] I ©2016 I Originally published under the title Sefer ha-histalkut in Tel Aviv in 1929 or 1930. I Includes bibliographical references and index.
Identifiers: LCCN 2016013095I ISBN 9781580238502 (pbk.) I ISBN 9781580238649
  (ebook)
Subjects: LCSH: Rabbis—Biography. I Hasidim—Biography.
Classification: LCC BM750 .M4413 2016 I DDC 296.8/3320922—dc23
LC record available at http://lccn.loc.gov/2016013095

10 9 8 7 6 5 4 3 2 1

Manufactured in the United States of America
Cover Design: Tim Holtz
Cover Art: © Brasiliao/Shutterstock
Interior Design: Tim Holtz

For People of All Faiths, All Backgrounds
Published by Jewish Lights Publishing
A Division of LongHill Partners, Inc.
Sunset Farm Offices, Route 4, P.O. Box 237
Woodstock, VT 05091
Tel: (802) 457-4000   Fax: (802) 457-4004
www.jewishlights.com

To my beloved, Phyllis,
for your love, your limitless support, and your wisdom.
שהא כמוך מי ימצא
A woman like you, who shall find
—J. B.

To my life partner, Michael,
who from the first time we met
was unafraid of death.
—S. P. O.

Contents

The Book of Departure

Contents

Contents

Foreword

Arthur Green

Torah means teaching. All of Torah is a course we take on the subject of how to live our lives. We sign up for that course in childhood, before we even understand why we need it, or what its subject matter is all about. Most of us ignore its wisdom much of the time, coming back to it only when life especially hurts or puzzles us. If we're very lucky, we turn back to it also in moments when we feel particularly blessed or filled with light. These moments, too, need the explanation we derive from Torah.

The Hasidic masters taught us that Torah exists not only in books but also in people. There are great souls in the world, scattered through every generation, who can teach us Torah by the way they live. We watch them and learn, edified by just being in their presence. Sometimes we are taught simply by the way they look at us, talk to us, listen to what we have to say. Some such people are *rebbes* or teachers to a whole community or even to the entire world. But others are teachers just to a particular person, perhaps someone they deeply love, or just in a particular moment, when the learner's heart is open to receive their truth.

Most of Torah's teaching is about how to live. But there is a special section within its wisdom that also speaks to us about how to die. Since we are all mortals, our lives fashioned somehow around the awareness that death is inevitably to come, this is one of the important lessons. We moderns are often too busy to heed it, or so frightened of turning toward it that we make ourselves "too busy." But our tradition, ever since our ancestor Jacob's deathbed blessing to his grandchildren at the end of the book of Genesis, calls us to pay attention. There is something profound to be learned about the way of dying, and it is best learned from the wisdom and stories of those who have gone before us.

Hasidic lore contains much of this wisdom. Its tales are studded with insights about death as well as life, all tied together in a single whole.

Hasidism is a deeply life-embracing strand within the fabric of Judaism. It teaches that this world, every moment and corner of it, is given to us as a setting for the uplifting of divine sparks, for the joyous service of God and celebration of the divine presence. The moments approaching death, even that of death itself, are a vital part of that service.

Some eighty-five years ago, a young immigrant to the Holy Land named Benjamin Mintz went through many volumes of Hasidic tales and teaching to collect the deathbed moments recorded here. He published them in Hebrew, in a modest volume with only bare explanatory notes. More than eighty years later, my student Rabbi Joel H Baron and his colleague Rabbi Sara Paasche-Orlow rediscovered this work and decided to translate it into English. As rabbis specializing in end-of-life care, they brought to it much wisdom of their own, tremendously enriching these tales with introductions and comments that bring the best of current practice together with these inspiring tales from another age.

What you have before you is a little gem of wisdom, simple but heart-touching deathbed tales from the Hasidic tradition, surrounded by thoughtful and inspiring reflections by contemporary practitioners. Whether you are a fellow practitioner in end-of-life care, the child or loved one of someone facing death, or just another mortal human seeking a bit of guidance and wisdom about the most eternal of questions, you have fallen into good and loving hands.

Introduction

R. Mordecai of Chernobyl asked him, "And where did you learn
that you could bring about salvation through storytelling?"
The saintly Rebbe of Ruzhin replied, "From our holy Torah!"
—Reuven Zak, *Kenesset Yisrael*

We are rabbis and chaplains who work with seniors living with health challenges, and we deal with death and dying—every day. Every one of our hospice patients is expected to die within six months; some, within days or hours. We care for Jews as well as people of all religious and non-religious backgrounds, the very old and the young old, those whose lives are rich with family and friends, and those who leave the world with no one there. How do we do what chaplains do—accompany those we serve—and come to that work from within a framework of meaning? We have learned a great deal about how to do this from Jewish *and* Christian colleagues, and from our patients, slowly coming to understand more about this time of life—and, indeed, it is a time of *life*. It will conclude with death, but it can be a time that holds and upholds a meaningful life in the context of that one individual and also among family, friends, and community.

In Abraham Joshua Heschel's great work *Torah min haShamayim* (*Heavenly Torah*), he studies the stories in the Mishnah, Talmud, and Midrash—as opposed to the more complex and traditionally studied legal material—as a way of gaining understanding about the nature of Torah and the ways in which God has been revealed to humankind. From Heschel we have learned new ways of approaching traditional Jewish literature so as to open a compassionate lens on that content with humanity at the center.

The Book of Departure—Sefer haHistalkut—is a book that brings together the end-of-life stories of forty-two holy men—*tzaddikim*—who died between 1760 and 1904, plus that of Isaac ben Solomon Luria Ashkenazi, the Ari, their philosophical forebear. Authored in 1930 by Benjamin Mintz, it was originally published in Hebrew in British Mandate Palestine. It has been our work to plumb the depths of those stories, to look into every corner of every sentence, and to try to understand the stories not only on their own but in relationship to each other as well. In this book we have attempted to bring our own experiences into conversation with those of the Hasidic masters who appear in these tales, and with our biblical, rabbinic, and intellectual forebears as well, and then to jump into the stream of conversation about death and dying. We do this in the hope that people of all backgrounds and faiths will gain insights and guidance when caring for the dying.

What Is Hasidism?

The Book of Departure is a collection of stories about the deaths of Hasidic rabbis. Hasidism is a popular and democratizing movement within Judaism that arose in the mid-seventeenth century in Eastern Europe. It is a form of Judaism that prioritizes one's personal relationship with God and accentuates ecstatic prayer as a fundamental aspect of the religious experience in addition to halachic, or "legal," observance and study. Through a populist form of Jewish mysticism, Hasidic Jews aspire to a life imbued with faith, joyfulness, and a profound sense of God's immanence.

Hasidism was centered around the teachings of Israel ben Eliezer (1698–1760), a *tzaddik* (righteous person) known as the Ba'al Shem Tov (or the Besht), and spread throughout the Pale of Settlement (those contiguous areas of Poland, Ukraine, Lithuania, and Belorussia where Jews were confined to live). The Hasidic movement gained momentum partially as a salve to the extreme disappointment that followed the false claims of Shabbetai Tzvi, a self-proclaimed messianic prophet, in the mid-seventeenth century; partially as a popular democratic alternative to the elite intellectualism of the mainstream rabbinic community in the seventeenth and eighteenth centuries; and partially as a communal healing following the Cossack Chmielnicki pogroms (the organized attacks against the Jews in May through November 1648) that utterly ravaged the Jewish communities of Ukraine.

The end-of-life stories in *The Book of Departure* all focus on leaders of this culturally and spiritually influential movement.

What Is a *Tzaddik*?

Not only is the text of *The Book of Departure* about Hasidism, but it is also almost entirely about the deaths of *tzaddikim*, or "righteous ones." In Hasidic Judaism, the concept of a *tzaddik* (pl. *tzaddikim*) assumed central importance as it evolved into an ideal religious personality. Reflecting the command in Deuteronomy 6:5, "And you shall love Adonai, your God, with all your *heart*, with all your *being*, and with all your *might*," the term *tzaddik* came to mean one who has attained such levels of self-mastery and spirituality that all thinking, all *feeling*, all *actions*—the *tzaddik*'s very *being*—are in total accord with God's will. This gives the person a uniquely close relationship with God. In essence, what distinguishes the *tzaddik* from anyone else is having an unparalleled command of the spiritual, which gives a person the ability to bridge the physical and spiritual worlds. Yet the most special virtue of a *tzaddik*—perhaps a *tzaddik*'s greatest strength—is to be the most human of human beings. A *tzaddik* can channel Torah into this world and give direction to others as to how best to serve God; the true *tzaddik* can take the most elevated aspects of godliness and bring them to a level accessible to all people:

> And over and over he takes you by the hand and guides you until you are able to venture on alone. He does not relieve you of doing what you have grown strong enough to do for yourself.... The [t]zaddik must make communication with God easier for his Hasidim, but he cannot take their place.... The [t]zaddik strengthens his Hasid in the hours of doubting, but he does not infiltrate him with truth, he only helps him conquer and reconquer it for himself.[1]

In his introduction to *The Book of Departure*, Benjamin Mintz tell us that the day of the death of a *tzaddik* is a moment for celebration because that death atones for the sins of the generation, because with that death harsh judgment departs the world, and because as the *tzaddik*'s soul rises it brings with it the many souls that have been awaiting repair and

redemption. The death of the *tzaddik* atoning for the sins of the generation is a known theme in Jewish thought as depicted in the Midrash:

> R. Abba bar Avina said, "For what reason was the verse of Scripture
> dealing with the death of Miriam (Numbers 20:1) placed close to
> that dealing with the ashes of the Red Heifer (Numbers 19:2)? To
> teach that just as the ashes of the Heifer effect atonement, so the
> death of the righteous effects atonement...."
>
> R. Chiyya bar Abba said, "The sons of Aaron died on the first of
> [the Hebrew month of] Nisan. Why then is their death mentioned
> in connection with the Day of Atonement (Leviticus 16:1) other
> than to teach that just as the Day of Atonement effects atonement,
> so the death of the righteous effects atonement.
>
> (*LEVITICUS RABBAH, ACHAREI MOT*, 20:12)

Thus we understand that the *tzaddikim* are valued not only for their
righteousness, but also for what they have the potential to do for
humankind.

Further, Hasidism teaches that those who recount the stories of these
deaths and who mourn for the departed *tzaddik* are also cleansed of their
own sins. Thus, as *The Book of Departure* recounts these final stories, giving us the details of the manner of the departure of each *tzaddik*, it gives
each of us the opportunity for spiritual renewal. In the *tzaddik*'s behavior at the time of departure "is reflected all the luminosity of his soul,"
and so, by examining those behaviors, we gain insights into their lives,
beliefs, and characters and are more prepared to recount and mourn
their departures. Exploring these deaths can also have a cleansing effect
on us as we find greater insight and spiritual meaning in facing death.
Perhaps we can let go of some of our fears and anxieties and find meaning such that we can be more fully present to others seeking our support
and, someday when we each face our own death, provide greater peace
to those we love.

In reading these stories we repeatedly see the place of the *tzaddik*
as unique in this world as well as in the world-to-come (the term used
to identify the Jewish idea of afterlife). The *tzaddik* exists for eternity
in realms reserved only for those who have achieved mythic levels of

righteousness. However, the exclusive status held by *tzaddikim* and the special eternal privilege allotted them is much less interesting than the potential for righteous character within each human being. There is an "inner *tzaddik*" to be encountered in every person; all are equal before God, and it is in that spirit that we read and find meaning in these stories.

The Afterlife

"It is clear that Jews believe many different things about life after death. However, when pressed for additional details on this topic, even among those who are well versed in Jewish thought, there is not a great deal more information forthcoming. Simply put, most modern Jews are vastly unaware of Jewish teachings on the afterlife."[2] Given this statement, how do we come to a Jewish understanding of the afterlife in the absence of a systematic theology on the topic?

One way is by utilizing narrative sources such as the stories that so clearly communicate a theology over and over in the pages of *The Book of Departure*. By listening to the teachings and stories of the rabbis, by plumbing the depths of the stories and the legal discussions in the Talmud, and by reflecting on all these sources, a richness of theological possibilities emerges. The soul's journey starting before birth appears to comprise three general stages: (1) preparation for life; (2) its experience in this world together with a body; and (3) a time of reward and resolution in the world-to-come, where it lives forever.

> The Lubavitcher Rebbe would often point out that a basic law of physics (known as the First Law of Thermodynamics) is that no energy is ever "lost" or destroyed; it only assumes another form. If such is the case with physical energy, how much more so a spiritual entity such as the soul, whose existence is not limited by time, space, or any of the other delineators of the physical state. Certainly, the spiritual energy that in the human being is the source of sight and hearing, emotion and intellect, will and consciousness does not cease to exist merely because the physical body has ceased to function; rather, it passes from one form of existence (physical life as expressed and acted via the body) to a higher, exclusively spiritual form of existence.[3]

Rabbinic sources say that after death the soul experiences the pain of separation from the body and undergoes the cleansing process of *Gehinnom* (a place of spiritual purification where the soul goes for up to twelve months following physical death). Further, immediately after death the soul is in a state of great confusion.

> The disembodied soul is intensely aware of the physical surroundings of its body. This is especially true before the body is buried. The soul then literally mourns for its body for seven days. This is alluded to in the verse, "His soul mourns for him" (Job 14:22)…. For the first 12 months after death, until the body decomposes, the soul has no permanent resting place and thus experiences acute disorientation. It therefore hovers over the body. During this time, the soul is aware of and identifies with the decomposition of the body.[4]

In Judaism, after death the soul may have the potential to achieve higher levels of *teshuvah* (repentance), piety, and closeness to God than it had been able to achieve in life. As separation from life is so difficult for the soul, at the time of death it wishes to be surrounded by those closest to it in life, yet, as we understand from the stories in *The Book of Departure*, once the soul has begun to depart, its attention may be focused in the world-to-come exclusively or perhaps both in this world and the world-to-come.

Whatever our individual theologies or world outlooks, one thing we may all be able to agree on is "this world is nothing like the world-to-come" (Talmud, *Berachot* 17a). Tempting though it may be, the purpose of this book is not to explore the full complexity of the rabbinic views (note the plural) of the world-to-come. In considering the topic, however, life after death and the ongoing life of the soul are core concepts. There has been much written and there is much to learn on this topic to expand our imagination, possibly deepen our belief, and certainly increase our understanding.

The Roles of Men and Women in Hasidism

Though these stories are dominated by men, we try to draw meaning for all people and a range of human experience, understanding that the rebbes mentioned here were part of a world that segregated men and women and where men had social and legal privilege. Additionally, all the students mentioned here are men. *Hasidut* (the teachings and practices of Hasidic Judaism) prior to the twentieth century followed the basic gender distinctions that segregated women from religious life, similar to the rest of the Orthodox Jewish world at the time. In Hasidism, women were not allowed around the rebbes' tables, and young men often left their wives and children behind to spend extended time with their rebbes in a spiritual family of men held together by the love of the rebbe. That said, the publication of some works in Yiddish, while done without the specific intention of including women, did allow women more access to some stories and teachings. And similarly, there are some exceptional women known for their learning. Some also hold that Hasidism understands itself as existing in an imperfect world while aspiring to an eternity where there is full gender equality.[5]

In the early twentieth century, in order to stop the rise of secularism, education of girls and women was established throughout much of Orthodoxy, including Hasidic sectors. The conceptual and communal structure, however, of women not assuming ritual leadership was still firmly in place. The stories that the reader will encounter in this work are thus almost exclusively about men; women are absent from the circles of students who surround their rebbes at the end of life. Keeping this pervasive gender critique in mind, *Hasidut* has still found a way to speak to us and influence greatly our postmodern world. Progressive Jewish life has embraced Hasidic *niggunim* (wordless songs), stories, and teachings. Also, through the open hearts and doors of the Chabad movement (Chabad is the largest Jewish religious organization in the world, well known for its outreach, particularly toward nonpracticing Jews) and the raising up of good will and good acts in the framework of an esoteric spirituality, Hasidism has outlived the impact of World War II, the decimation of Eastern European Jewry, and what many considered seeming irrelevance in the postwar rise of secularism and has influenced the spiritual heart of twenty-first-century Jewish lives.

However, we still found ourselves peering into the shadows of the stories looking for the missing women, and we have included comments where *tzaddikim* are known to have had prominent mothers, sisters, and daughters. Our hope is that by reading our twenty-first-century male, female, and gender-sensitive lives into our interpretation, we succeed in making these texts relevant to more people without excluding anyone. In the act of reading these stories, it is our purpose to raise the sparks that can illuminate our lives today and allow all to be brought into community around a rebbe's table. To this end we seek to find relevance in these stories today for people of all backgrounds and orientations.

The Structure of This Book

In searching for a pathway into the subject of Jewish pastoral end-of-life care, we began studying *The Book of Departure*. It was written—perhaps "edited and introduced" would be more accurate—in 1930 by Benjamin Mintz. Mintz, born in 1903 in Łódź (in today's Poland), studied in a Hasidic school. He immigrated to Mandate Palestine in 1925 and worked in construction and as a printer. He was a founder of Young Agudat Yisrael, which began as the original umbrella party for almost all ultra-right-wing religious Jews in Israel, and he was later a member of the Provisional State Council. In 1949 he was elected to the first Knesset (Israel's Parliament) and was reelected in 1951, 1955, and 1959. In 1960 he was appointed minister of postal services by David Ben-Gurion, serving until his death the following May.

Mintz's subtitle for *The Book of Departure* is *The Paths of Departure of the Righteous in the Hasidic Tradition, from the Ba'al Shem Tov until His Later Students.* This unique recording of end-of-life stories was passed down orally and eventually written down by the students or the students of the students of these rebbes. Mintz condensed the Hebrew text in some places and improved the Hebrew in others. Though a few of the individual stories have been translated into English, the work as a whole had not been translated. For those interested, the full Hebrew text can be found at www.daat.ac.il/daat/history/hasidut/sefer-2.htm. As we began studying the text, with its references to Bible, to a host of rabbinic texts, and to the great Jewish mystical work the *Zohar*, we began to unpack the texts and extract their meaning and application for caring for all people at the end of life.

By approaching the end-of-life stories of these rabbis as narrative theology, by following the pathways into the texts to which the stories refer, and by extracting modern pastoral lessons, we aspire to help people make meaning out of the experience of caring for others at the end of life and to expand the boundaries of life such that we as community members can help to enrich and foster spiritual depth up until our loved ones and we ourselves breathe our last breath.

First, of course, the text needed to be translated, and it is our hope that the present translation will be one of the contributions of this work. *The Book of Departure* is a collection of stories that appeared individually in other works; the value of this book is not only the collection itself, but also in Benjamin Mintz's introduction to it. This bringing together between two covers of the last moments of life of these *tzaddikim* offers the reader the possibility to learn from these rebbes about how to live fully and most thoughtfully right up to the end.

The Hebrew text throughout this book is most probably a recording of stories that were told orally in Yiddish. Hebrew was not a spoken language among the Hasidim, as it was considered a holy language reserved for sacred texts, a *loshen kodesh*. As these stories recount the ends of life of holy people, it would have been appropriate to write them in Hebrew. Alternatively, it is possible that they were first written down in Yiddish and then translated by Mintz or people before him.

In this text, we have tried to use accessible language. We have used Hebrew words only when it is critical to understanding the intent of the text. For example, the Jewish observation of the seventh day is called *Shabbat* and is observed from one hour before sundown on Friday until darkness on Saturday. But Shabbat is more than a day of the week; it is also a concept: a twenty-four-hour period with a full body of laws, literature, and lore that surround it. Calling it by its English equivalent, the Sabbath, denies the word the context in which it existed for the characters in these stories. Nonetheless, even when we have made the decision to use the Hebrew, we have always translated it into English, and the reader will find a collection of these words and concepts in the glossary that is found at the back of this book.

The Stories

"Why is it that telling the story carries the same healing power as the original act? Because the story recreates the act in such a way as to invite us into it. We don't simply listen to a story; we become the story. The very act of giving our attention to the story gives the story a personal immediacy that erases the boundary between the story and ourselves."[6] So it is with the Hasidic tale; these stories, whether you understand them to be factual or allegorical, have not only become a way for us to understand the history and theology of the Hasidim, but they have also become a tool for helping us understand our own histories and belief systems—and they have provided us with new ways of understanding the ways we help care for people at the ends of their lives.

Part of our love of working with elders is that there is little artifice; they tend to be unguardedly insightful about their lives and the challenges they face. When they pray as individuals or in community, they bring their vulnerability, raw yet seasoned emotion, love, pain, and the individuality of a lifetime of experience. This is true of these stories as well. As we approach death, there is less time for small talk; each word becomes pregnant with meaning, and the essence of the individual shines through.

There may have been diverse versions of the written stories of the ends of the lives of the rabbis included in this work. For the sake of bibliographic accuracy for those interested in pursuing these stories from their original sources, we have provided a complete list in Hebrew along with the full Hebrew text of *The Book of Departure* online at www.daat. ac.il/daat/history/hasidut/sefer-2.htm.

Navigating This Book

1. **Notes and Comments** are used extensively in the book, outside of the main text of the story, to give readers an uninterrupted flow as they read, leaving explanations to the side. There are two types of notes: (1) numbered items that provide the reader with source, linguistic, or straightforward explanatory content; and (2) comments marked with the symbol ⟨≈⟩, where we more fully develop the pastoral lessons to be taken from *specific* words or phrases that

have been boldfaced in the text; and which provide *general* discussions of issues raised in the story.

2. **Insight Sparks**, which appear throughout the text, are brief essays, nineteen in all, that go into greater depth on larger topics that one way or another seem to provide an underpinning to many if not all of the stories. We explore such topics as blessing the children, clinging to God, coping with dementia, ethical wills and advance directives, kindness, and the timing of death itself. It is our sincere hope that our exploration of these topics will help deepen all of our understandings of the issues that arise in this study. As your own thinking and understandings develop, we would love to hear from you at DeathbedWisdom@gmail.com.

Jewish End-of-Life Practices

As various aspects of Jewish practice at the end of life are referred to throughout this book, it seems prudent to spend some time providing the reader with a brief overview of the various practices associated with tending to those we love as they approach death. When a person is in an active dying process, Jewish tradition refers to him or her as a *goses* (a dying person) and once dead as a *met/metah*, as the state in which the body is prepared for placement in a casket and then the burial itself.

1. During the final moments of life, we are guided by tradition to remain and watch over the person as he or she passes from this world to the next.

2. There is a tradition to recite a confessional prayer at the end of life (called the *Vidui*), if possible while a person is still cognizant. This moment of life can be a time of affirming love, forgiveness, and togetherness. On the days following the *Vidui*, it can be meaningful to continue to say the *Shema* together, which traditionally was prescribed as a person's final words. The *Shema* prayer, "Hear, O Israel, Adonai is our God, Adonai is One," is found in Deuteronomy 6:4. Further, it is a tradition to recite psalms next to the person until the moment of passing and afterward as well.

3. While the most traditional sources say that one should not touch or disturb the person at all for fear of hastening death, it is

common and appropriate for people who share an intimate relationship, such as a spouse, sibling, child, parent, close friend, or grandchild, to touch the person gently, hold a hand, or lie in bed next to the person and hold him or her if this will offer comfort.

4. After a person dies, a doctor or nurse will remove any medical devices, and it is incumbent on the oldest child (if present) to close the person's eyes, place the hands palms up next to the body, and cover the person with a sheet.

5. It is difficult to express in just a few words the ultimate respect shown the body of the deceased. Those preparing the body even ask the dead person for forgiveness if in any way they have caused him or her distress. Appropriate prayers are recited; the body of the deceased is cleaned and washed, purified in a simple traditional manner, and clothed in the simplest of cotton or linen garments, resembling those worn by the High Priest when he entered the Holy of Holies (Exodus 28:39–43, 39:27–29).

6. The principle that governs the care of the body immediately following death is the sacredness of the human being. "A human being is equated to a Torah scroll that is impaired and can no longer be used at religious services. While the ancient scroll no longer serves any useful ritual purpose, it is revered for the exalted function it once filled."[7]

7. Immediately following a death until the moment of burial, according to tradition, the deceased should not be left unattended; the body should not be abandoned prior to its arrival in its new "home" (Talmud, *Berachot* 18a; *Shabbat* 151b). (Traditionally, Jewish burial takes place as soon as possible, preferably within twenty-four hours of death, but can be slightly delayed for a number of practical reasons.) Further, the understanding is that the soul hovers over the body for three days after death. The human soul is somewhat lost and confused between the time of death and burial and so stays in the general vicinity of the body until it is interred.[8] Therefore, a *shomer*, "a watcher," stays with the deceased, reciting psalms, poetry, or other literature or liturgy, thus comforting the body, the soul, and the surviving loved ones as well.

8. Finally, the body is washed, blessed, and dressed in shrouds, called *tachrichim*. This process is called *taharah*, and is done by the *chevra kadisha*, the Holy Society, according to traditional customs. A large plain cloth (a *sovev*), a prayer shawl, and a special belt are placed in the casket. One of the fringes of the prayer shawl is cut to signify that it will no longer be used for prayer and that the person is now absolved from having to keep any of the commandments. Lastly, the body is placed in the casket, the belt is tied, and the prayer shawl is wrapped, as is the outer cloth. Soil from Israel is sprinkled in the casket ("For dust you are and to dust you shall return," [Genesis 3:19]). The casket is permanently closed, as it is not Jewish practice to open a casket for viewing.

9. Again, a *shomer* stays with the body, protecting and accompanying him or her until the time of the funeral and burial.

In Conclusion

We live in an aging society. Therefore, we need to be prepared to engage in thoughtful decision making and planning for ourselves, together with those we love, as we and they approach the latter years and months of life. Further, a great deal is being written—and will continue to be written—trying to understand the ethics of end-of-life medical care. Much of that writing is driven by the moral and ethical teachings of America's many religious traditions. As we grapple with these great moral questions, we have the opportunity to turn to Hasidic masters, to bring those writings into conversation with important modern voices as well—be they ethicists, healthcare professionals, rabbis and chaplains, or politicians.

This book seeks to contribute to the spiritual lives of elders as they near the time of death and also to the lives of those who care for them. We hope to bring new perspectives, guidance, and support from these Hasidic stories as well as from our own learning experiences and insights.

The Book of Departure

Introduction to
The Book of Departure

Benjamin Mintz edited *The Book of Departure: The Paths of Departure of the Righteous in the Hasidic Tradition, from the Ba'al Shem Tov until His Later Students* in 1930, when he was twenty-seven years old, five years after he moved to British Mandate Palestine. He gives no clue in this introduction as to why he assembled this work. There is a reason in the tradition as to why he might have stopped with forty-two stories.

In the section of the Torah called *Parashat Mas'ei* (Journeyings), the closing section of the book of Numbers (33:1–36:13), Moses recounts the "departure points" of Israel during its forty-year history after leaving Egypt, that is, he records each of the places where they encamped and set up the *Mishkan*, the Ark of the Covenant, on their journey to the Promised Land. All told, there were forty-two such departure points, and so our stories number forty-two as well, providing us with a journey through the desert of seeking understanding about dying and death such that we can hopefully help others and ourselves add meaning and opportunity to our final days. Mintz may also be pointing us to a belief that in death we also arrive in a Promised Land.

As *The Book of Departure* is a book of stories about *tzaddikim*, the exploration of the importance of their deaths is the subject of Mintz's introduction. We also refer the reader to the broader discussion "What Is a *Tzaddik*?" found in our introduction to this book. What follows here is Benjamin Mintz's introduction to *The Book of Departure*.

The most deeply honored day of all days in the opinion of the Sages is the day of death—even more important than the day of birth. And if this is said of ordinary people, how much more so

(continued on page 5)

1   Mishnah Avot 4:17.

≈   **hiding ...** Warm food that is buried (see note 2 above)—"hidden"—to be kept warm for Shabbat is explicitly warm, but we also can understand that at the right time it will be unburied in order to nourish us. So, too, the body of the *tzaddik* after death is called "hidden"; so, too, all of our bodies. Tradition tells us that we are buried—hidden—to be recalled in the flesh when the Messiah comes, this time for eternal life, for the ultimate mutual nourishment of the body for the soul and of the soul for the body.

2   As the word *hatmanah* ("hidden") is used for the procedure of burying food on Shabbat in order to keep it warm, the use of this word implies a "temporary burial," which we have translated as "hiding."

3   *Genesis Rabbah, Parashat Vayechi*, 96:4 on Genesis 47:29—"'And the days of Israel (Jacob) drew near to die.' Resh Lakish said, 'By your life! You will lie down, but you will not die, for it says (in Scripture), "And the days of Israel drew near to die."'"

4   Like Jacob in the preceding sentence, Enoch was also a *tzaddik*, among the nine righteous men who, according to *Derech Eretz Zuta*, a post-Talmudic tractate, entered paradise without suffering the pangs of death. Enoch is first identified in Genesis 5:24 in the listing of the generations of Adam. The midrash on that verse, *Genesis Rabbah* 25:1, says that God "took" Enoch "while he was [still] a *tzaddik*," implying that he was inclined to do evil, so God took him before he died—thus Enoch lived out his days *walking* with God. Here, Enoch's departure is used as evidence that the soul of a *tzaddik* may die, but his soul is with God forever.

5   Again, a text that underscores the Hasidic notion that the soul of the *tzaddik* lives on—only his body dies. Later in the text we will learn that this can be true for all people. Here the reference is from the *Zohar*, part III, *Acharei Mot*, 57a. The Hebrew text used by Mintz is not a direct quote from the *Zohar*, rather an adaptation of the original Aramaic.

6   Jerusalem Talmud, *Yoma* 2a. Here, Aaron, a *tzaddik*, is likened to the tablets themselves—his death was as hard for God as was the shattering of the tablets of the Ten Commandments on Mount Sinai.

of the *tzaddikim*! For them the day of death is turned into a day of celebration.

For *tzaddikim*, we don't [use the term] "death" at all; [we only speak of] "a departure" from this lowly world and a rising up to the world-to-come. The soul departs from the body, the spirit from the material—and the *tzaddik* ascends to higher rungs. Because of this, [on the one hand] the *tzaddik* longs for the day of death all the days of his life and prepares himself for this great day, even though, on the other hand, he wants to keep this day far off. For did they not say, "Better is one hour in repentance and good deeds in this world than all of life in the world-to-come"?[1]

Death of *tzaddikim* is also referred to as "a lying down," "a **hiding**,"[2] or "a sleeping," and it is a matter more precious than death, and about this they said, "Jacob our father did not die, but the blessed Holy One said to him: 'By your life! You will lie down but you will not die.'"[3]

And this is the meaning of what it says regarding Enoch, "And he was no longer, for God had taken him."[4]

And in the *Zohar* it says, "*Tzaddikim* die a death of their body; their soul does not die."[5]

The departure of the *tzaddikim* from this world is the subject of many rabbinic teachings, from the ancient Sages of the Talmud through the later kabbalists. On the one hand, there is sorrow over "death" in general and the death of *tzaddikim* in particular, while on the other hand—on the positive side—a beautified image of death is given to us: Good is brought for the one who has departed and good [is brought] for the world. They said, "It is difficult for the blessed Holy One to decree death upon the *tzaddikim*, and the death of Aaron (the *tzaddik*) was as difficult for the blessed Holy One as when the tablets were shattered."[6]

(continued on page 7)

7 The parenthetical "a *tzaddik*," is Mintz's addition to the original quote, which comes from *Yalkut Shimoni*, a thirteenth-century commentary on the books of the Bible, here specifically on Ecclesiastes 7:1.

8 Ecclesiastes 7:1.

9 *Zohar*, part III, *Acharei Mot*, 56b.

10 Isaiah 6:7.

11 "Soul-root" in kabbalistic thought is that place where one's soul becomes one with God (see *Tanya*, chapter 2).

〜 **in this behavior is reflected all the luminosity of his soul ...** Of course, not everyone gets to die a comfortable, easy death where this luminosity is apparent. Some die suddenly, and some suffer with extended dementia. Some who die with advanced dementia may exhibit personality changes and no longer resemble the person people knew before. At these times it can help to remember the finest qualities a person once had, the luminosity of that soul, and hold those in our heart while accompanying the person in the moment.

〜 **the death of Moshe Rabbeinu ...** There is a process of such sweetness and tenderness surrounding the death of Moses at the end of Deuteronomy that it has created a model for us to emulate as we tend to those who are dying. The Rabbinic literature is replete with comments on this process, but perhaps it is the deep love between Moses and God that is the basis for the model we need to follow (see also Ginzberg, Volume III).

〜 See Insight Sparks: Dying on an Auspicious Day; The Language of Death.

They also said, "When a person (a *tzaddik*)[7] dies, everyone should rejoice and offer thanks that he departed with a good name and that he left this world in peace. This is what Solomon said: 'The day of death [is better than] the day of one's birth.'[8]"

The death of *tzaddikim* sometimes comes because of the sins of the generation, and it always atones for them. (And thus it is said, "Whenever *tzaddikim* depart from the world, harsh judgment departs from the world.") Moreover, as it rises to the uppermost worlds, the soul of the *tzaddik* raises with it the many souls that have been waiting for *this* soul a long time—in order to be repaired and to bring them to their supernal roots.

And not only does the death atone by itself, but all who tell of the death of the *tzaddik* and are sorrowful about it, their sins are also atoned for: "The blessed Holy One said, 'Turn your attention to the death of these righteous ones, and it will be considered as if you were bringing offerings to atone for yourselves.' ... When anyone feels sorrow over the loss of the righteous ... the blessed Holy One proclaims for him, 'Your iniquity is removed, and your sin purged.'[9, 10]"

Because of this, the manner of the departure of the *tzaddik* is important to us—each according to his rank and his soul-root[11]—so will be his behavior at the time of the departure and in his last moments of life in this world. Sometimes **in this behavior is reflected all the luminosity of his soul**.

The books of the Sages are full of descriptions of the departures of *tzaddikim*. Especially wondrous *and* soul shaking is the description of **the death of Moshe Rabbeinu**. Also the description of the death of R. Shimon bar Yochai is filled with awesome splendor.

In this book I am intending to give a handful of the paths of departure of the *tzaddikim* who lived close to our own times—from the Ba'al Shem Tov up to his latest students in spirit, as provided to us in the Hasidic tradition, but I precede these with a short description of the departure of the late Ari, of blessed memory, who is considered the spiritual master of the students of the Ba'al Shem Tov.

1 *Kohen* (pronounced ko-HEYN; pl. *kohanim*) is the Hebrew word for "priest." *Kohanim* today are thought to be descendants of Aaron, the first High Priest in the Hebrew Bible, brother of Moses and a member of the Levite clan. Priests needed to remain in a state of purity in order to perform the ritual sacrifices required in the Temple, and long after the Temple was destroyed, they were traditionally still required to remain pure. According to Jewish law, they are still today not permitted to be in a room with a dead body, which is considered a primary source of impurity. This explains the Ari's insistence later in this story that R. Yitzchak the *Kohen* leave the room before the Ari dies.

2 The student may be looking for a respectful way to recognize the fact that "great good and Torah and wisdom" have *not* been established in the world, and he is challenged by his rebbe's impending death. It's almost as if he's saying, "Is this it?"

~ **If I had found ...** When the Ari says, "If I had found even one complete *tzaddik* among you, I would not depart," it is as if a person can choose not to die. Alternatively, he may be saying that he would have lived on in the teachings of the right heir or disciple, since one's ideas and values can live on through students and through children.

3 The Ari does not respond directly to the question asked, but responds by saying that there is no one yet available to pick up his mantle, and goes on to say that he will continue to teach them—from the world-to-come—until one emerges in this world to become a new teacher. It is interesting that though the Ari is the spiritual forefather of Hasidism, the next *tzaddik* important enough to be included in this work is the Ba'al Shem Tov, the founding rabbi of Hasidism, who was born 164 years after the Ari.

~ **And where has R. Chaim Vital gone ...** The roles of Yitzchak the *Kohen* and Chaim Vital are interesting to highlight. Yitzchak, the loyal student, risks his purity status as a *kohen* to be with his teacher and asks only one thing: How can he continue to learn from the Ari after the Ari's death? He doesn't complain that it is not he who will have the secrets imparted to him; he merely stands by waiting to serve his teacher. Nor does he complain when his master wishes to see a student other than him. In the face of death he expresses incredible humility.

4 Chaim ben Joseph Vital (b. 1542) was the foremost disciple of the Ari and recorded much of the Ari's teachings; it is not unlikely, therefore, that the Ari would be disappointed not to have him by his side at the time of his death.

The Ari—Isaac ben Solomon Luria Ashkenazi

Isaac ben Solomon Luria Ashkenazi (1534–1575), known as "the Ari," was a leading rabbi and mystic in Safed in what was then Palestine. His name "the Ari" means "the Lion" in Hebrew and is an acronym for the Hebrew of "the Holy Rabbi Yitzchak." His Lurianic Kabbalah is foundational to contemporary Jewish mysticism. In this story, the Ari invites us—future generations of learners—to be among those who gather at the bedsides of the *tzaddikim* the reader will meet in the ensuing pages of this book. In furthering these stories we join those who have been worthy of carrying on the learning and evolving understanding of matters beyond our physical lives. The rest of this book comprises the stories of the rabbis in whom the soul of the Ari lives on.

When the Ari was actively dying, may his memory be a blessing, all of his students stood around him with the exception of R. Chaim Vital. R. Yitzchak the *Kohen*[1] came in and wept before him and said, "Is this all that we hope to be established by your life—seeing great good and Torah and wisdom in the world?"[2]

The Ari responded, "**If I had found** even one complete *tzaddik* among you, I would not depart."[3]

Afterward the Ari asked, "**And where has R. Chaim Vital gone** at this time?"—and he was very distressed.[4]

(continued on page 11)

5   Kabbalists—Jewish mystics—believe that only certain people, those who have achieved the highest levels of learning and practice and have an understanding of a mystical unification with God, are appropriate for further study of mysticism. The great book the *Zohar* is considered the central text of Jewish mystical belief.

6   As in a daydream.

7   As a descendant of a priestly family he is not permitted to be in proximity to a corpse. But also, the Ari is telling him to go be who he is: "Be who you are, a *kohen*, not who I am." This evokes the famous story of R. Zusya, who says, "In the coming world, they will not ask me, 'Why were you not Moses?' They will ask me, 'Why were you not Zusya?'" (Buber, 1:251).

〜   **in a kiss ...** Death in this image nullifies the division between the soul and God—returning the soul to the divine Self (Fishbane, 127). Thus, a person can fulfill Moses's command that is evoked regularly in the first paragraph of the *Shema* prayer ("Hear, O Israel, Adonai is our God, Adonai is One"), to "love Adonai your God, with all your heart, with all your being, and with all your might" (Deuteronomy 6:5). And so, the memory of God's kiss that ended Moses's life is a model for all times; God takes the lives of all the *tzaddikim*, and possibly all people, with a kiss. God is thought to take our soul from us at the end of our lives and then returns that soul to us in the world-to-come, with a kiss—a symbol of love and unification.

8   Rashi (Rabbi *Shlomo Itzchaki*), a prominent commentator on Torah who lived in the twelfth century, offers an explanation for how Moses died, as described in Deuteronomy 34:5, "And Moses the servant of Adonai died there, in the land of Moab, by the mouth of Adonai." Rashi says that "by the mouth" means "with a kiss"—as God breathed life into the Adam at Creation, so God's "kiss" took away Moses's earthly life.

〜   See Insight Sparks: Blessing the Children; Body and Soul; The Timing of Death.

R. Yitzchak the *Kohen* understood from the Ari's words that he most probably had in mind to transmit a secret to him. Afterward R. Yitzchak asked the Ari, "What shall we do from now on?"

The Ari said to him, "Say to our friends in my name that from today onward they should not occupy themselves with the particular wisdom of Kabbalah, because they do not understand it properly and could be led, God forbid, to heresy and even lose their souls. Only R. Chaim Vital should engage with it, and even then, quietly and in secret."[5]

And his students asked, "And so, God forbid, there is no longer hope for us [to study Kabbalah]?"

He said, "If you will merit it, I will come and teach you."

R. Yitzchak the *Kohen* asked him, "And how would our Rabbi come to teach us once he has departed from the world?"

The Ari said, "You have no business with the secret ways of my coming, whether in a dream, while awake,[6] or in a vision. Now, get up quickly, go from this house, for you are a *kohen*[7] and the time [of my death] is approaching, and there is no time to go on at length about anything."

And he left quickly, but before he had crossed the threshold, the Ari opened his mouth and his soul went out **in a kiss**.[8]

He was released on the fifth of Av, 5335 (July 22, 1575).

Body and Soul

For *tzaddikim,* we don't [use the term] "death" at all; [we only speak of] "a departure" from this lowly world and a rising up to the world-to-come. The soul departs from the body, the spirit from the material—and the *tzaddik* ascends to higher rungs.

—Benjamin Mintz, introduction to *The Book of Departure*

In Rabbinic thought, the soul is pure. It is always pure because it *always* belongs to God. We learn from Talmud, "Just as the Holy One, blessed be God, fills the entire world, so too the soul fills the entire body. Just as the Holy One, blessed be God, sees but is not seen, so too does the soul see, but is not seen…. Just as the Holy One, blessed be God, is pure, so too is the soul pure" (*Berachot* 10a).

While we live, the Rabbis teach, the soul unites with our body, but still it is God's. And, just as the soul itself returns to God, many will seek a fundamental place for comfort as they approach their own final departure.

Psalm 146:4 teaches, "His spirit is departing, he [i.e., his body] will be returned to earth; on that day his thoughts are lost." What does this mean? "His spirit *is departing*" is written in the present tense, so we can assume that the soul begins its departure first. Nothing is said of the duration of that departure, but the Rabbis will have something to say about this later on.

"He will be returned to earth" reminds us of Genesis 3:17–19: "Cursed be the ground because of you; by toil shall you eat of it all the days of your life…. By the sweat of your brow you shall eat bread until you return to the earth—for from it you were taken. For dust you are, and to dust you shall return." Our bodies return to the earth and become dust. The soul's return to God is active and present; the body's decomposition is passive and future. The departure of the soul seems immediate; the body's destiny is at some unspecified time in the future.

And what of "on that day his thoughts are lost"? The text seems to relate to the idea that when we die all our thoughts, ideas, and memories—all of our mental imaginings—die as well. Thus, according to Psalms, while our soul is eternal, our individuality as we know it today disappears with death.

As the stories in *The Book of Departure* unfold, they seem to reveal a Rabbinic sense of a fine scrim that separates this world from the world-to-come, with the timing and process of the soul leaving the body existing quite separately from the death of the body. As the body begins to die, the soul begins to rise up and begin the process of its final joining with God. "In the world-to-come there is no body or physical entity, only the souls of the righteous alone, without a body, like the ministering angels" (Maimonides, *Mishneh Torah, Hilchot Teshuvah* 8:2).

Many people toward the end of their lives will reach out to their family, seek God, or recall a tradition that gave meaning at some time in their lives—all of these represent acts that may help them remain intact in the face of highly reduced control of their own lives. If we assist the dying in making peace with their lives and connecting to the eternity of their own souls, it may give them something to hold on to, whether they believe in the soul and God or not. If they can believe in the future of their own souls, if they can believe even in their own goodness and the value of their lives, perhaps they will find greater peace.

~ **On *leil Shavuot* ... his chosen people were gathered close to him ...** At the end of the Ba'al Shem Tov's life, during the night of the holiday of Sha-vuot (the Feast of Weeks, also called Pentecost), his students were gathered around him, which is also the case for many of the *tzaddikim* included in *The Book of Departure*. In Torah, we are told that Abraham, Ishmael and Isaac, Jacob, and Aaron and Moses are all "gathered" to their people at the end of their lives. Thus, since people gathered around them at the ends of their lives and it is used with a sense of finality, the language hints at a gathering both in this world and in the next world as well.

The Hebrew term translated as "his people" includes his family, his stu-dents, and those in his broader community. This is particularly relevant in our modern world where a person may define his or her people in many different ways; the important idea here is that he or she is gathered to those who are closest and to the eternity and community of Jewish peoplehood.

Having said that, as we observed above, we must remember that some people nearing death may need us to limit our time with them and to help them limit the number of people who can visit. In the opening sentence of this story, the Ba'al Shem Tov retreats to his meditation room in order to be alone, perhaps to begin his preparation for his own death, perhaps to begin separating himself from his Hasidim so that they and he can begin to practice a life without his physical presence.

1 It is likely that he is teaching the traditional Torah reading for the festival of Shavuot, which is about the giving of the Torah (Exodus 19–20). Almost presaging the Besht's death, the reading says, "Moses ascended to God, and Adonai called to him from the mountain, saying, 'So shall you say to the house of Jacob and tell the sons of Israel; you have seen what I did to the Egyptians, and [how] I bore you on eagles' wings, and I brought you to Me'" (Exodus 19:3–4).

2 The Hebrew, *yitasku*, implies the tending to his physical body. See also "Jewish End-of-Life Practices" in the introduction to this book.

The Ba'al Shem Tov

R. Israel ben Eliezer (1698–1760) is generally acknowledged as the central figure of Hasidic Judaism. He is referred to as the Ba'al Shem Tov, the "Master of the Good Name," the explanation of which is given by Martin Buber as "one who lives with and for his fellow-men on the foundation of his relationship with the Divine" (Buber, 17). The little biographical information we have about the Ba'al Shem Tov (he is also referred to as the Besht, an acronym for *Ba'al Shem Tov*) is so interwoven with stories of his life and of miracles he is alleged to have performed that myth has blended with history.

When he became sick before his "departure," the Ba'al Shem Tov did not lie down on a bed, rather he had become frail and his voice was stricken, and he was sitting by himself in his meditation room.

On *leil Shavuot*, the final night of his life, **his chosen people were gathered close to him** and he taught about the giving of the Torah.[1] In the morning he sent for them that all of them should gather, and he gave them instructions on how to care for him after his departure.[2]

(continued on page 17)

≈ **"I will speak a bit more with *Hashem*"** ... There is a powerful message here about spontaneous prayer, that is, prayer specific to a situation and created in the moment. Jews are accustomed to prayers that are written down in prayer books, as it is our mandate to pray in community, and fixed prayer can help us find expression for our thoughts and emotions and remind us of important aspirations. It can become a path for the flow of our prayers and can bring us into unity with others who are praying simultaneously. Many of us, however, have also learned to pray from our hearts—to speak directly with God and develop a practice of spontaneous, unformatted prayer. When people are dying, depending on their own spiritual backgrounds, they and their families may take comfort from familiar prayers, but at times they might also be comforted when that prayer is created in the moment in response to their unique situation—in both cases, prayer is offered from the heart.

3 "Speaking with God" is the way Hasidism understands prayer, which exists on a very intimate footing. R. Nachman of Breslov says, "When God helps with *hitbodedut* [a practice of seclusion wherein one communicates with God] it is like a person talking to his friend" (*Likutei Moharan* 2:99). For a person with a developed prayer life, trying this practice when alone may prove very satisfying—speaking as one would to one's most intimate friend, about everything. For more on this topic, see also Azamra.com, www.azamra.org/Essential/hisbodedus.htm.

≈ **Angel of Death** ... The Besht lived with an awareness that the Angel of Death was pursuing him. From the moment he was born that pursuit began, and as he lay near death, he was aware that the angel was hovering over him, waiting for the decree from above that would give the angel permission to take the life from the Besht's body. Some of us may also live with a constant fear of death, and it may be comforting to connect with the Hasidic belief that our souls go back to God; the Angel of Death—also God's agent—takes only our body back to the earth.

4 That is, he's always chased him away.

5 Ecclesiastes 8:8. In the Bible the usual translation and understanding of the verse is that "one has no authority *over* the day of death," meaning that no one can choose the day of one's death; here it is translated "one has no authority *on* the day of death," expressing not having personal autonomy during the last day of one's life.

Afterward he instructed them to give him the prayer book, and he said, "**I will speak a bit more with *Hashem*,** may He be blessed."**3**

Later, they heard him saying, "I concede those two hours to you. Do not bother me." And they asked him with whom he was speaking, and he said to them, "Don't you see the **Angel of Death** that was always fleeing from me?**4** And now that he has been given permission over me, his wings are spread and it is a great joy for him."

After all the people of the city had entered [his room] to greet him on the holiday, he [the Ba'al Shem Tov] recited words of Torah.

Afterward, at the time of the meal, he instructed his attendant to put honey on a big saucer, but he brought it on a small one. And he said, "'One has no authority on the day of death,'**5** even the *gabbai* [the person who coordinates the synagogue services] doesn't obey me."

(continued on page 19)

6   Is he speaking here to the Angel of Death, the people of the city, or to his *gabbai*? The implications of each could be quite different. Nonetheless, he is telling those around him that this time—the time of dying—is one when he needs *chesed*, loving-kindness.

7   To help them stay focused with him in life, the Besht is reassuring them that the moment of his death will be clear to them and that until then they can be fully present.

~   **so that it could not be seen …** The Ba'al Shem Tov is well aware of his approaching death, but his students may think they can protect him from that knowledge and that doing so is good for him. Indeed, neither is possible here, as he knows exactly what is happening. In general, many dying people are well aware of what is happening and possibly have accepted it, but the loved ones surrounding the dying person may have not yet arrived at acceptance. It is important at these times to help family, friends, and other caregivers so that they can support the person dying to be at peace and can bring love and not anxiety into the room.

8   He is caring for his followers here. While they are trying to protect him from seeing that the clock has stopped—that he is going to die—he clearly understands that he is actively dying whether he can see the big clock or not. Yet he can assure them that he is all right and prepared to die—prepared because he knows that his soul will enter the world-to-come. In the next paragraph he launches into his final teaching to them about the nature of the departure of the soul to eternal life. And in his final moment he asks them to recite a psalm of comfort for him, the life force drains out of him, his soul departs, and his body dies.

Afterward he said, "Until now I have acted with loving-kindness toward you; now it is time for you to reciprocate."[6]

And he offered them a sign, that when he would be released [i.e., when he would die], the two clocks of the house would stop.[7]

He washed his hands and the big clock stopped and the people turned it around **so that it could not be seen**, and he said to them, "I am not worried about myself, because I know clearly, that I will leave through this door and immediately enter through another door."[8]

(continued on page 21)

⟦∿⟧ **he spoke words of Torah to them …** As the Ari was teaching mystical secrets at the end of his life, so the Ba'al Shem Tov is teaching Torah at the end of his, and Jacob in the Torah also gave his wisdom at the end of his life. We see this action repeated over and over again in these stories. This transmission of knowledge is a gift we can give to our loved ones, and we can communicate our deepest values, as these ancestors are modeling for us.

9 "He spoke words of Torah to them: about the pillar through which one ascends from the Garden of Eden below to the Garden of Eden above." The Besht, said to have been born in 1698, may well have been aware of the book *Ma'avor Yavok* (1626) by the kabbalist Aaron Berechiah ben Moses of Modena, who teaches, "He will command unto you channels of lights that are appointed over the departing soul so that the soul will not be troubled in its departure, that God forbid, death be decreed upon it." The book describes the process of entering the higher world of life as a reflection of the soul's experiences while within the body. *Ma'avor Yavok* is a primary source document for the prayers that are used by *chevra kadisha* groups (burial societies) when they prepare a body for burial and includes customs and rituals pertaining to the sick, dying, and dead in the light of various kabbalistic texts.

10 The original Hebrew for the preceding is expressed as a complex abbreviation that traces its roots to the *Sefer Yetzirah*, the *Book of Formation*, the earliest book on Jewish esotericism, in the acronym *a-sh-n*, which represents holy space, holy time, and holy souls, the *tzaddikim*.

11 The words *Vihi Noam* ("And may God's pleasantness be upon us") begin the closing verse of Psalm 90. This verse, together with all of Psalm 91, compose the *Vihi Noam* prayer, a prayer recited multiple times in succession by kabbalists to ensure God's protection.

12 *Kavanot* are "intentions" or "directions of the heart," which when recited are thought to help people align themselves spiritually with God.

13 Literally, "they could not hear him cutting letters any longer."

And he sat up on his bed and instructed them to stand around him, and **he spoke words of Torah to them**: about the pillar[9] through which one ascends from the Garden of Eden below to the Garden of Eden above, and thus between each and every world how this symbolism manifests in holy space, time, and people,[10] and in the way in which it is realized in worship. And he instructed them to recite *Vihi Noam*,[11] and he lay down and sat up a few times and practiced *kavanot*[12] until they did not hear him articulating words any longer.[13]

(continued on page 23)

≈ **cover him with a sheet ...** He asks to be covered with a sheet. Is he cold? Does he feel the chill of the Angel of Death approaching, is the sheet granting him some solitude, or is it to keep the sight of his dying from those around him? Today, people are often lying in bed covered at the time of death, and we cover them entirely, including their head, with a large piece of cloth, a *sovev*, when they have died. After ritual cleansing, dressing, and preparation of the body (see "Jewish End-of-Life Practices" in the Introduction) are performed, the tradition is to wrap the body one final time.

≈ **he began to shake and to tremble ...** The Yiddish word for this rocking movement is *shuckeling* (literally, "to shake"), a constant rocking back and forth, which one might consider as a "movement meditation" and is believed to increase concentration and emotional intensity. In Hasidic lore, *shuckeling* is seen as an expression of the soul's desire to leave the body and unify with the Source (see *Tanya*, chapter 19). Perhaps the addition of "trembling" has to do with a physical response to the departure of his soul. In such cases today a hospice nurse might administer small amounts of morphine to help a patient whose number of breaths per minute has reached uncomfortably high levels and is appearing to be in a state of discomfort.

He asks for his prayer book and is praying the *Shemoneh Esrei*, or Eighteen Blessings, the standing prayer that is the very core of a Jewish prayer service, at the very end of his life. Praying in these final moments or reciting the *Shema*, a declaration of faith, is an oft-repeated event in these stories, an event that seems to hold the moment or possibly create a bridge between worlds for the dying person.

≈ See Insight Sparks: The Angel of Death; Kindness; Meditation; Purity; The Timing of Death; The Language of Death.

And he instructed them to **cover him with a sheet** and **he began to shake and to tremble** as when [davening] the *Shemoneh Esrei*, and afterward he rested a little bit. And they saw that the small clock had stopped. And they waited a while, and they saw that he had departed.

He was released on Shavuot (sixth of Sivan) 5520 (May 16, 1760).

The Angel of Death

"I concede those two hours to you. Do not bother me." And they asked him with whom he was speaking, and he said to them, "Don't you see the Angel of Death that was always fleeing from me? And now that he has been given permission over me, his wings are spread and it is a great joy for him."

—From the deathbed story of the Ba'al Shem Tov

So many of us live with a consciousness of death in our daily lives. We thank God or simply breathe a sigh of relief when a friend, spouse, or child returns safely home from a trip or returns to health after an illness. Death resides at the margins of daily living, leaving us grateful after driving through difficult weather, when a child walks home safely through the city, when an elderly parent lives another healthy day. At times we easily embrace a positive relationship to the fragility that we call life, and at other times, particularly after loss, we strive to hold on to a sense of security. Jewish tradition creates many paths, concepts, and structures to help us with this and to reach peaks of good emotion as well. In our daily prayers, the *Ashrei* prayer, which is the most recited prayer in the service, is all about affirming our happiness and God's greatness and securing our ongoing role in this world.

The Angel of Death as portrayed here is a striking metaphor for this daily presence. When a person is very old and potentially faced with terminal illness, a change often occurs. Death can become an intimate presence, which is accepted by some and constantly traumatizing to others. And for those who might feel acceptance, it might still evoke deep sadness and possibly a range of emotions. The expression "Pneumonia is the old person's friend" is the closest we might come in our American culture to acceptance of a welcome death, because it evokes painless dying as an end to suffering. Pneumonia in this context, when untreated, often allows a person to enter a state of reduced consciousness and die peacefully in his or her sleep, allowing for a calm and untroubled end often after a period of suffering and illness.

The name "the Angel of Death" evokes this tension between possible good in the midst of necessary bad. We hear "angel" as a protective and calming notion, but when partnered with death it evokes fear. As a person nears the end of life, as with the Besht, our work together is to approach death without fear and with a sense of love and protection.

~ **completely separated from this world** ... There can be a moment when a person's soul has already left the body and gone to the world-to-come, or, in other words, when the conscious self is gone, even as the physical body still registers signs of life force. This can be a very confusing time, and it is important to continue to behave and remain attentive to the fact that hearing is the last sense that people lose and the dying person may still be aware on some level of what's being said, even without the ability to respond.

1 If we knew this man today we might think him consumed with "fits of madness," delirium, or dementia, but clearly his students didn't see him that way; they were more apt to understand him the way we might think of prophets going into ecstatic states as they receive the word of God. In Numbers 11:26–30 we have the story of Eldad and Medad: "And the spirit rested upon them ... and they spoke in ecstasy in the camp" (11:26). In the first paragraph of the story, the rebbe's students understand that his soul was cleaving to God much as the spirit might rest upon a prophet, and they watch over him lest his soul's "great cleaving with the Creator" be completed and he pass into the next world, which is what happens at the end of the story. In the second paragraph, we see the rebbe in a near frenzy as the time of the third meal (i.e., late afternoon) approaches. Perhaps this is an intense moment of ecstasy; perhaps it might also be related to mental illness or is due to "sundowner's syndrome." Sundowning is a psychological phenomenon associated with increased confusion and restlessness in people with some form of dementia; the term refers to the fact that a range of behavioral problems often begins to occur in the evening or while the sun is setting. Many patients with dementia will experience some sort of sundowning confusion. As the rebbe's ecstasy subsided, one of his children would eat the meal with him, and then they would go to synagogue for prayer and study. In this story we possibly see people managing mental illness or dementia in an elder and an attempt to find the sacred in an otherwise tragic situation.

R. Yechiel Michel of Zlotshov

R. Yechiel Michel of Zlotshov (ca. 1721–1782) was a prodigy who was introduced to the Ba'al Shem Tov at a very young age. Zlotshov is the name of a Hasidic dynasty founded by R. Yechiel Michel and is the Yiddish name of Zolochiv, a town in present-day Ukraine.

Two years before his departure R. Yechiel Michel of Zlotshov was already **completely separated from this world**, and it was necessary to watch over him so that his soul would not leave from its great cleaving with the Creator.[1]

(continued on page 29)

~ **the third meal** ... A rebbe sitting with his students at the third meal, the *seudah shlishit*, has special significance. It was this meal that drew together all the Hasidim of the town around the *tzaddik*'s table as it began to get dark. It was then they felt most keenly the sanctity of Shabbos, and that was the time when the *tzaddik* gave his major Torah expositions. "The Hasidim believed that the souls from 'the World of Truth' come to hear the Torah of the Tzaddik at this meal" (Wertheim, 227–28).

Another tradition teaches that on Shabbat we are given an extra soul. We don't really know what this means, but it can be experienced in the feeling that in this special time of Shabbat it is not just the day of the week that is different but we are somehow different as well. We are told that this extra soul enters on Erev Shabbat and begins its departure at the time of the third meal (*Keter Shem Tov* 2:21). When this second soul leaves, when the end of Shabbat is drawing near, and the burdens of the week begin to return, we have to let go of Shabbat, and also a part of ourselves slips away and is lost. This loss of the second soul at the close of Shabbat imparts to us a small foretaste of death. In the lingering singing of the third meal, the sacredness of Shabbat has been building even as it nears its end and is now peaking with intimacy and a sense of profound peace and longing. In Shabbat we find a metaphor for the final chapter of life, the rest at the end of a long and full week.

2 Of the three commanded meals on Shabbat (Talmud, *Shabbat* 117b), the third meal has been given special significance in Hasidic communities. The tradition of celebrating the third meal is carried out with great enthusiasm and singing, sometimes continuing hours after Shabbat has officially ended.

3 This reference to "the fierce and the impetuous" is the borrowing of a phrase from Torah, where it is used to describe the enemies of Israel, and it is used here to describe the fierceness and intensity of the experience of the day on which the rebbe died.

4 The reference to the day "on which the Ark of God was taken" is twofold. First, in the biblical story (1 Samuel 4:18–22) the Philistines capture the Ark, and upon hearing the news, Eli the priest falls back and dies, as R. Yechiel is about to do, and it becomes a day of mourning. Second, the metaphor of the Ark "being taken" also applies to the death of a *tzaddik*, who is sometimes referred to as a "holy ark" (see also "R. Menachem Mendel of Vitebsk," "The Seer of Lublin," and "R. Shlomo, the *Kohen* of Radomsk"), and evokes a sense of holiness departing from the world.

His habit was to pace back and forth in his room until his face was burning like a torch of fire, and then it was necessary to watch him very closely. And it was also his habit to eat **the third meal**[2] in his room with one of his sons, and afterward he would go to the house of study to recite Torah and songs and praises.

And on this day of Shabbat—a day of "the fierce and the impetuous,"[3] on which the Ark of God was taken,[4] at the time of divine

(continued on page 31)

5   Next in the story we have the expression "the time of divine yearning," *b'et rava d'ravin*, an Aramaic expression we see repeatedly in these stories. A good translation might be "at the time of the yearning of the yearning one." It describes what happens when God is feeling an intensity of *desire* or *will* at an ending. It describes that particular desire to hold on to something special right at the time that it is about to end—in this case, Shabbat or a lifetime.

6   Finally, at the end of the third paragraph, our rebbe is alone in his room repeating, "Through this will Moses departed." This is a quote from the *Zohar*. According to tradition (Talmud, *Sotah* 13b), Moses died on Shabbat afternoon, thus it is traditional to recite this verse about his death at the third meal, which is what R. Yechiel is doing. The verse evokes God's love and a spirit of joy rather than judgment regarding Moses's death: "But on Shabbat when the time of the *Minchah* service arrives [i.e., the late afternoon], the divine will appears, and the Holy Ancient One reveals this will. All judgments are suppressed, and favor and joy pervade everywhere. Through this will, Moses— holy, faithful prophet—departed from the world in order to demonstrate that he did not depart by judgment.... Happy is the share of Moses" (*Zohar*, part II, *Yitro*, 88b).

〰   **shook him to extract him from his cleaving ...** His son attempts to extract him from his cleaving, from dying, but instead his father dies. It may seem that once a person is actively dying there is no turning back, but often we cannot predict when the end will come, and at times a person will rally, granting us a few more hours or days of connection, but most often not, as in the case of R. Yechiel.

7   That is, upon reaching the last paragraph of the last word of the *Shema*—"One."

〰   See Insight Sparks: Coping with Dementia; Liminality.

yearning[5]—no one was there with him in the room. And he was running back and forth shouting, "Through this [divine] will Moses departed. Through this [divine] will Moses departed."[6]

His daughter heard, and she sought out her brother R. Isaac of Radvoyel. He (the brother) ran to his (R. Yechiel's) room, he grabbed him and **shook him to extract him from his cleaving** [to God], but, alas, he fell upon his shoulder, calling out *Shema Yisrael*, and his soul departed at *echad*.[7]

He was released on the third of Nisan, 5542 (March 18, 1782).

Coping with Dementia

Two years before his departure R. Yechiel Michel of Zlotshov
was already completely separated from this world.
—From the deathbed story of R. Yechiel Michel of Zlotshov

We are the "People of the Book," proud of our learning, our focus
on education, and of all the brilliant and creative Jewish people who
have invented, studied hard, and worked hard as part of a culture
that is always pushing forward. We are also a tradition grounded in
chesed, loving-kindness, embracing the stranger and caring for the
downtrodden.

It can be the hardest moment in life to face the onset of dementia or
to watch parents or beloved elders who have been sharp and discerning,
reflective and wise, or in their own way a genius, as they begin losing
that connection to intellect. How do we adjust and feel love and blessing
for ourselves and for those we love, even as we change and suffer deep
losses in our identities? It is a lifelong task to honor the simple humanity of being, to address every person, including ourselves, as worthy, to
find that point of connection and deep identification with the other and
offer relationship and love.

We want to share the story of a musical and intellectually gifted elder
named Leah who was able to find wholeness as her identity shifted and
waned. Leah was born into a large family that came to America to escape
the pogroms in the years leading up to the Holocaust. They were observant Jews, and her father was a locally renowned scholar. When Leah
as a young adult married a man who was forced to work on the holy
Sabbath in order to create a business and support his extended family,
it was devastating for Leah's father. When her father wrote his Torah
commentary, it was dedicated to all of her seven siblings, and her name
was missing. She had literally been written out of "the book." This was a

lifelong tragedy for Leah, and yet she kept it hidden deep inside. As she aged and began to see some signs of dementia in herself, she needed desperately to be written back into the book: the Book of Life, of continuity and eternity. In telling her story and in feeling supported and cared for as she witnessed her own loss of self, she was able through music and prayer to find peace.

We don't know exactly what occurred with R. Yechiel, but we do know that it was honored and guarded by his students, and in particular we hear mention in this story of his children. It can be the hardest for children to accept changes in their own parents; tradition understands this and makes allowances for others to be engaged to help. But in this link between generations, whether children or students, or simply a younger generation, we need to keep in mind that we *do* have the power to write each other into the Book of Life.

[1] These men were all members of the rabbi's group of some forty disciples.

[~] **were standing before him ...** Again, at the end of life, a *tzaddik* is being "gathered to his people" and is passing along his most important life lessons. With this string of four instances of "And afterward," we witness great love, affection, and compassion in the farewells to each of his "sons," urging them to stay together as a "family" once he's gone. In these blessings he addresses three different kinds of love: companionship ("you will be with me"), longing ("I will truly long for you"), and a physical, concerned taking care of ("I will take care to take you out of your troubles"). So as caregivers, we too may be called upon to understand the relationships between the dying and those close to them by understanding each of these modalities and by responding to the subtleties of each.

[2] These words are a quote from Job 23:13—the sense in Job is that God is everywhere and God's will is inevitable.

[3] Founder of a Hasidic dynasty; he died in 1800. He is also called Zusha; the town is also called Anipoli.

[4] So begins a series of private moments with each of those close to him. He is not only taking care of them in these moments, saying something reassuring and personal to each, but he is also affirming the connection that will go on after his death.

[~] **you are mine in this world ...** The statement "You, Zishe, you are mine in this world and you will be with me there [i.e., in the world-to-come] as well" attests to the rabbinic understanding of a thin wall between this world and the next. They seem to believe that the next world is more than a continuation of this world—not everyone will be with him, but Zishe will be, possibly implying that Zishe will die sooner. This is a common sentiment between longtime spouses whose lives are so intertwined that it seems evident that they will somehow continue to be together in death as in life.

R. DovBaer of Mezritch

R. DovBaer ben Avraham of Mezritch (the Maggid of Mezritch; ca. 1710–1773) was the primary disciple of the Ba'al Shem Tov, and the key leader in the emerging Hasidic movement. R. DovBaer is regarded as the first systematic exponent of the mystical philosophy underlying the teachings of the Ba'al Shem Tov, and through his teaching and leadership—he was undoubtedly the main engineer of the movement—Hasidism began spreading broadly following his death. Indeed, most of the leading Hasidic dynasties stem from his disciples and his descendants. Within fifty years of his death the majority of the Jews in Ukraine, Galicia, and central Poland were Hasidic and sympathetic to Hasidism, as were substantial minorities in Belarus, Hungary, and Romania.

Before the departure of the great Maggid, R. DovBaer of Mezritch, his son, R. Avraham "the Angel," R. Yehudah Lib the *Kohen*, and R. Shneur Zalman, the Rav from Liadi,[1] **were standing before him**.

He said to them, "My sons, hold yourselves together as one, and thereby you will overcome everything, go forward and not backward, and," as alluded to in the verse, "'God is One; who can dissuade God?'"[2]

And afterward, R. Zishe of Hanipoli[3] also came, and he (DovBaer) signaled to him with his finger to come over to him—and he came.[4] He took him by his right hand and said to him, "You, Zishe, **you are mine in this world** and you will be with me there [i.e., in the world-to-come] as well."

(continued on page 37)

5 Menachem Mendel of Vitebsk (1730?–1788) was in the third generation of leaders of Hasidic Judaism. He was a primary disciple of the Maggid of Mezritch, and in the winter of 1772 he, along with R. Shneur Zalman of Liadi, went to the Vilna Gaon with the aim of convincing him to rescind his ban on Hasidism, but the Gaon would not receive them. After the Maggid's death, R. Menachem Mendel, along with three hundred other followers of the Maggid, immigrated to Israel (Palestine), settling in Safed. The *Tanya* is partially based on his mystical works.

6 Malachi 2:7. This is excerpted from a stinging rebuke of the priests given by Malachi, and while stated in a positive light, it is here also clearly a warning to his disciple. A fuller quote from the text (Malachi 2:7–9) reads as follows: "For the lips of a *kohen* guard the knowledge of Torah, and men seek rulings from his mouth; for he is a messenger of Adonai of Hosts. But you have turned away from that course: You have made the many stumble through your rulings; you have corrupted the covenant of the Levites—said Adonai of Hosts. And I, in turn, have made you despicable and vile in the eyes of all the people, because you disregard My ways and show partiality in your rulings." R. DovBaer takes a positive statement out of this negative rebuke, by the very last of the prophets in the Bible, and uses it as a gift to his disciple—raising up a spark at the end of his life.

7 Particularly in the early mystical period, there was a focus on the relationship between the heavenly and earthly realms. In this story we see the earthly priest—the one who is a keeper of the knowledge of Torah—and the Maggid, who is soon to be heavenly keeper of the knowledge of Torah, saying that he will guard R. Yehudah Lib from there as well (Elior, 755).

And afterward he asked if R. [Menachem] Mendel of Vitebsk[5] was there, and Shneur Zalman responded that he was not. And DovBaer moaned greatly.

And he asked if R. [Yehudah] Lib the *Kohen* was there, and he looked at him and said to him, "You, too, will be with me, 'for the lips of a *kohen* guard the knowledge of Torah,'[6] and I am from the world of knowledge [of Torah]."[7]

And afterward he said—in these [very] words, "Zalmaneh, Zalmaneh! You will remain on your own, but I will take care to take you out of your troubles, for I will truly long for you."

(continued on page 39)

8 R. DovBaer's son Avraham (1739–1776) committed himself to an ascetic and secluded lifestyle. When his father died, he did not assume his father's leadership position even though he was held in high regard by all of his father's main disciples, and he died within several years of his father.

9 Now he is speaking to the only one of his students—his "sons" as he calls them all—who is a biological son. The Maggid may understand that Avraham is excessively hard on himself and wants him to go easier so that his life will go easier, or perhaps the father is telling his son not to feel bad that he has named R. Zalman as his successor. In the sweetness of the tone with which he addresses his son, the last person with whom he speaks before he dies, he is proving his love and affection as a father, above and beyond his role as a great teacher.

≈ **his merit will protect us ...** This phrase attests to the belief that the power of a person's righteousness extends "protection" to those closest to that person, even after death. This concept between generations stems from the older notion of the merit of the patriarchs and matriarchs, the ancient idea that the pious deeds of Abraham, Isaac, Jacob, Sarah, Rebecca, Leah, and Rachel secure blessing for the current generation. When God gives Israel the Ten Commandments, the giving is accompanied by the promise that "God shows kindness to the thousandth generation of those who love Me and keep My commandments" (Exodus 20:6). This idea, that the goodness of a person's life can continue to have good effect in the world, and realizing this through giving *tzedakah* (i.e., "charity") in the person's name, may help the bereaved still feel a closeness to the deceased.

≈ See Insight Sparks: Blessing the Children; Body and Soul; Kindness.

And afterward he said, "Avrahamneh,[8] you should live [and be well], you should only keep quiet and behave yourself like [you have up] until now and comply with Zalmeneh, *he* should live [and be well]—and it will be good for you. But the main thing is that you shouldn't torture yourself, because if we make a small hole in the body we make a big hole in the soul, and is your soul not entirely special?"[9]

And he said, "Good night," and he slept—**his merit will protect us**.

He was released on the nineteenth of Kislev, 5534 (December 4, 1773).

≈ **aspects of his soul ...** It is an amazing gift to many families and friends when older people begin to record—by writing, film, or audio—their deepest beliefs and what they want to pass on to those they love and have influenced in their lives. For some individuals these messages might be obvious, as they, the individuals, have lived them so clearly; other people might need to provide greater clarification. Here, R. Elimelech, the person who is credited with beginning the broad dissemination of Hasidism, is taking this to a higher level by concretely charging his disciples with aspects of his soul, his character, which they then must carry on. At the end of people's lives it can be easy to lose sight of their character because they have dementia, are in intolerable pain, or simply are not gracious about aging; with others, their essence might become more clear and distilled through the passage of years. Families might be following the culture and beliefs of an elder or might have rejected or turned away from that life and its values. It is common, however, to hear a person remark that one of the grandchildren has his or her grandparent's integrity or sense of humor and that another has the grandparent's stubbornness. Whether through deeply held beliefs, character traits, or lessons learned, these are all ways we can experience the eternity of a life, challenging the finitude of human experience.

≈ See Insight Sparks: Ethical Wills and Advance Directives; The Timing of Death.

R. Elimelech of Lizhensk

Elimelech Weisblum of Lizhensk, Poland (1717–1786), was one of the great founding rebbes of the Hasidic movement. He was part of the inner circle of DovBaer of Mezritch, the second leader of the Hasidic movement, becoming one of the third-generation leadership after the death of R. DovBaer of Mezritch. He was particularly influential in his articulation of the figure of the *tzaddik* and is the author of *Noam Elimelech*, a book of commentaries on the Torah in which the role of a *tzaddik* is set out and explained, while the doctrine of Hasidism is explained in greater detail. The book was the subject of an intense investigation by the *mitnagdim*, the opponents of Hasidism.

When he was approaching his time to depart from this world, R. Elimelech of Lizhensk placed his hands on the heads of his students, and to four of them to whom he was closest he distributed **aspects of his soul**.

To the Seer of Lublin he gave the light of his eyes; to the Maggid of Koznitz, the strength in his heart; to R. Mendel of Prostik, the soul that was in his brain; and to the Rav of Apt, the strength that was in his mouth.

He was released on the twenty-first of Adar, 5546 (February 19, 1786).

1 It is a custom to add the name Menachem, which means "comforter" or "consoler," to the name of the fifth month of the Jewish year, Av, calling it Menachem Av. Av is a month that is known for tragedy because in this month both the First and Second Temples were destroyed. Adding "Menachem" here evokes consolation, and the consolation of generations comes to bear also on the impending loss of the beloved rabbi. The scroll of Lamentations is read on the ninth day of the month of Av, Tisha b'Av—the day on which the destruction of both the First and Second Temples was said to have occurred. In Lamentations 1:9 we read, *Ein la menachem*, "She has no consoler," suggesting that though we seek consolation we do not always find it. The addition of "Menachem" in the name of the month also brings attention to the meaning of the name of the rebbe being discussed and honors his compassionate qualities.

2 That is, he died. The hiding of the "holy ark" is a metaphor for the death of a rebbe, beginning with the death of R. Yehudah haNasi (see also "R. Yechiel Michel of Zlotshov," "The Seer of Lublin," and "R. Shlomo, the *Kohen* of Radomsk").

R. Menachem Mendel
of Vitebsk

Menachem Mendel of Vitebsk (ca. 1730–1788) was mentioned above as a key disciple of R. DovBaer of Mezritch. He was part of the third generation of Hasidic leaders and instrumental in spreading Hasidism throughout Belarus (White Russia). In the winter of 1772, he went to the Vilna Gaon with the aim of convincing him to rescind his ban on Hasidism, but the Gaon would not receive him. In 1777, he led the first Hasidic group to immigrate to the Holy Land, settling first in Safed and later in Tiberias. His teachings, which emphasize *deveikut* (see "Insight Spark: Clinging to God") as the ultimate goal of religious life, became part of the basic framework and content of the *Tanya*, the main work of the Chabad philosophy.

In the month of Menachem Av[1] 5547 (1787) R. Menachem Mendel of Vitebsk became ill with the sickness from which he died. And he [tossed and] turned on his bed many days in his sickness until Rosh Hodesh Sivan 5548, when the [holy] ark was hidden.[2]

(continued on page 45)

⟨∿⟩ **he no longer seemed human ...** Given how strong the rebbe's spirit and mind still were, and his body so diminished, it was as if they were experiencing a being of pure spirit, no longer inhabiting his shell of a body, and yet still present in this world. At the end of life people may be physically diminished and no longer appear like the person we knew. This story teaches us to see beyond their physical diminishment and be able to experience them in a time when they have surpassed the physical. That said, it can be painful to see someone we love transformed in this way and then struggling for each breath when death is imminent. Jewish tradition is very clear on two points: one, that we treat the dying person as a fully live person, and two, that we treat the body after death with the utmost care and respect. Even though we might barely recognize the vital person we once knew, and we might even be yearning for death to happen so that they do not have to exist like this, we are taught to remember that this is still a person created in the divine image, and it can be helpful to recount the actual biblical verses: "And God said, 'Let us make an Adam in our image, after our likeness.... And God created the Adam in His image, in the image of God He created it; male and female He created them" (Genesis 1:26–27). The fact of our being created in God's image is repeated four times in two verses, finally punctuated with a statement making it clear that this image is true for all humanity, not just Adam. In a situation where the caregivers find themselves wishing for imminent escape for the one dying, it may be helpful to recall the beginning of life, the pain and vulnerability of birth, and to see God and Creation in the person before them.

He suffered terribly, and he was so wasted and thin that **he no longer seemed human**. Still, his mind was strong, his teaching clear, and he chose his words with a settled mind and sparkling logic, until the final chapter.

(continued on page 47)

⟿ **God is standing above me!...** If we understand that God stands above a patient, it can help us consider where to stand or sit. Where is our place in this three-way relationship? What is our relationship to God at this moment? What is our relationship to the dying person once God is so near? What do we feel about being a part of these relationships?

⟿ **God is standing above me!...** Dying patients often have visions when they are actively dying. Some may see God; some, angels; often people see loved ones who have died before them. It is fine to acknowledge these visions, understanding that they are truly what the person is seeing and experiencing. (See also the appendix, "The Characteristics of Active Dying.")

3 The Talmud teaches that the Shechinah, God's presence, stands above the head of the bed of a sick person, and so the rebbe doesn't want anyone "standing in the way": "The Divine Presence stays above the bed of a sick person; as it is written, 'Adonai will sustain him on his sickbed' (Psalm 41:4)" (Talmud, *Nedarim* 40a). It can be very comforting to feel that when one is in such a weakened and vulnerable state, not knowing what lies ahead, that God is there close by, like the cloud that accompanied the Israelites in the desert, providing shade and a sense of accompanying presence on their journey.

4 The son continues learning from the father right up until the end, which is signaled by a final sweat. The word for "sweat" stands out here in the text because it is used in only one place in the Bible. In the beginning of Genesis we read, "By the sweat of your brow shall you get bread to eat, until you return to the earth—for from it you were taken. For dust you are and to dust you shall return" (Genesis 3:19). The allusion to a final sweat and thus to Genesis is meaningful because this death is quite different from the others in this collection, as the rebbe speaks of God's presence but does not invoke the afterlife. Rather, the story signals a return to dust by referencing the presence of the rebbe's sweat.

⟿ See Insight Sparks: Clinging to God; The End of Desire.

Shortly before his departure he warned those standing over him, "Depart, please from above me, because now **God is standing above me!"**[3]

After a brief moment they returned to him and they approached, and from time to time he spoke until the final sweat[4] fell upon him. And his son asked him about the sweat—what it was and what was its nature. And he replied to him, "Hush, as it is the end of everything!"

And amid these words, he passed—and his righteousness went before him.

He was released on Rosh Hodesh 2 of Sivan, 5548 (June 7, 1788).

Clinging to God

Afterward he spoke further words of Torah with great joy and a wondrous conjoining [with God] until all those standing around him were astonished and amazed.

—From the deathbed story of R. Shneur Zalman of Liadi

The Hebrew word *deveikut*, which can be translated as a "clinging on to" or "cleaving to" God, communicates an almost physical "joining with" God that can be achieved during prayer or study or even while going through the actions associated with living daily life.

Deveikut is a concept that has taken on richer and richer meaning over the centuries, as it has come at times to communicate an ecstatic and intimate connection with God. It also has strong roots in the Torah itself, where we find the root of the word *deveikut* fourteen times. Our first encounter is in Genesis, where the narrator says, "Therefore, a man leaves his father and his mother and *clings to* his wife" (2:24). And later, in Deuteronomy 4:4, Moses reminds the Israelites, "But you, those who have *clung* to Adonai, your God, all of you are alive today." It expresses both physical and ideological union.

During the time that Hasidism was forming, traditional Rabbinic Judaism was preeminent, and it was believed that the common folk were not capable of achieving *deveikut*, because it had taken on intellectual overtones as well. The Ba'al Shem Tov challenged that mentality and taught that believing, common folk could become as close to God as a traditional scholar. Thus, we find repeated references to *deveikut* throughout the Hasidic literature (see "R. Yechiel Michel of Zlotshov," "R. Shneur Zalman of Liadi," "R. Aaron of Zhitomir," and "R. Shmuelke of Sasov").

The End of Desire

On Friday, on the [eve of the] holy Shabbat, before his departure, he was very weak and he was vomiting much blood and had almost expired, and his students stood before him. His principle disciple, R. Nathan, pleaded, "Rabbi, please save yourself." He answered, "I have no desire."

—From the deathbed story of R. Nachman of Breslov

How do we answer when a very sick or very old person has been suffering—in this case of R. Nachman, vomiting blood—and they say they no longer have a desire to live? It is easy, like R. Nachman's student, to want to argue and say, "Think of us who need and want you to live," or to give reasons for life being important. In the moment you hear from someone that he or she no longer wishes to live, search inside yourself for a time when you really felt like life was no longer worth living. Allow yourself to tune in to those emotions without speaking. Inhabit that place with the person who is indeed inching closer to death. To accompany is not about pulling a person back from the brink but is more about standing *with* the person *on* the brink and being able to experience together the view from that vantage point. Fulfilling the mitzvah of *bikkur cholim*, visiting the sick, requires the awareness that our places could be switched, and it is with this spirit, a completely equal stance, that we truly encounter another person, and in that meeting place his or her full humanity is honored, upheld, and protected from diminishment. It is this very togetherness—this sense of alignment—that can counter the existential notion that ultimately one dies alone.

1 For a fuller presentation of this story, see Green, 275–82.

~ **while one is still clothed in a body ...** This communicates the Hasidic idea that in life a person can achieve only certain levels of piety but after death has the potential to achieve even higher levels, to develop an even greater closeness to God. There are many different reasons why a person might feel that he or she needs to move beyond this life. We are reminded of a man who as he approached one hundred years of age understood and could speak about the ways in which his death would allow for an expansion in the lives of his sixty-something-year-old children. Here was a man who had the strength of character that allowed him to look at a world beyond his own finitude. Other people speak with longing about joining a spouse or loved one who has predeceased them.

2 See also "R. Yitzchak Yoel of Kantikuziva."

3 The symbol of a ladder presented here recollects Jacob's dream where angels come and go from the heavens (Genesis 28:10–17) and adds complexity with the visual of the rebbe being at the very top, and yet before in his life there were always further opportunities to advance. The notion of never staying on one rung but holding on to and standing on multiple rungs at the same time—as when climbing a ladder—presents a picture of dynamic growth in R. Nachman's life. In our own lives, when we pursue spiritual growth and attempt to understand life and our relationship with the Divine, we too climb a ladder of personal reflection, introspection, and learning. Indeed, when we stand on a ladder, it is most often not with two feet on the same rung or two hands on the same rung, but with each of the four on a different rung. It is this state of reaching that characterizes the lives of certain people and becomes less possible as a person nears death. Like R. Nachman, such people often are seeking new avenues to advance up until the moment of death. The idea of not being able to advance while still clothed in a body seems to signal an advanced spiritual state where R. Nachman is yearning to be free of the physical experience.

R. Nachman of Breslov

Nachman of Breslov (1772–1810), a great-grandson of the Ba'al Shem Tov, was the founder of the Breslov Hasidic movement. He breathed new life into the Hasidic movement by combining Jewish mysticism with in-depth Torah scholarship. He has become one of the most influential of the Hasidic rebbes, with a religious philosophy centered on closeness to God and speaking to God "as you would with a best friend." The concept of *hitbodedut* (a form of prayer and meditation) is central to his thinking.[1]

Some months before his departure R. Nachman of Breslov said that he was already standing on such a [high] rung that it was impossible to go any higher by any means **while one is still clothed in a body**, and he said that he was very much longing to strip away his body [from his soul].[2] Because it was not possible for him to stay on [only] one rung under any circumstances, and all the days of his life he had never stayed on [just] one rung even when he reached whatever high rung it was—even the highest imaginable—when he would get to that rung he would do something even newer until he would reach a higher and then an even higher rung.[3]

(continued on page 53)

~ **he began looking for a burial place for himself ...** This is the first of several stories in this book where people select their own grave. In this story we are led to the mystical view that the location of the grave of a *tzaddik* may have an impact on healing the world and, further, to understanding that we live and die in community and our death and burial can impact our community. Finding a place for burial or a thoughtful plan for how our remains will be managed can sometimes help our loved ones feel our love and support even after we are gone.

4 When he selected Uman as his burial place, he was referring to the cemetery of the town where many Jews had been buried following the massacre of Jews and Poles at Uman in 1768. During Nachman's lifetime, thousands of Hasidim traveled to be with him for his teachings on Rosh Hashanah and other holidays, but on the last Rosh Hashanah of his life, Nachman emphasized the importance of being with him for that holiday in particular. Today, in response to this teaching, tens of thousands still make this annual pilgrimage to Uman each Rosh Hashanah.

5 The Sabbath of Comfort, the Shabbat immediately following the observance of Tisha b'Av, the ninth of the Hebrew month of Av. This is again the same root as the name Menachem that we noted in the previous story.

6 "R. Nachman himself, one of the most spiritual of all the zaddikim, felt a deep and secret sense of union between himself and 'simple men.'" This affinity is the point of departure for his statement two months before he died that he was a now "a simple, ordinary man." At first he was in a very weak state, but then he suddenly went over into an elated and inspirational time, and Martin Buber explains that "in such periods of descending, the *zaddik* was infused with vital strength which poured out from him into ... all people" (Buber, 7).

The words "a simple, ordinary man" are a translation of the Yiddish word meaning "common" or "plain," even "rough." The point of him mentioning his simplicity here is that he is about to die and he has lost his vigor and charismatic presence, but not his universal humanity, and this is followed by a period of almost ecstatic teaching.

A long time before his departure **he began looking for a burial place for himself**, because, for reasons he kept to himself, he didn't want to repose in Breslov, and ultimately he chose Uman because he said that several repairs [to the world] depended on it and that there were many secrets that it was not possible to reveal.[4] By the time he had settled in Uman, he was already very weak.

And on Shabbat Nachamu[5] many Hasidim gathered near to him, and before he washed his hands for the meal he said, "Why is everyone here! Don't you all know that now I am a man who knows nothing special? Now I am just a simple, ordinary man."[6]

(continued on page 55)

7   He has been speaking from the ninth of Av until the seventeenth of Tishrei, a total of sixty-seven days.

8   In other words, his disciple is saying, you have the power to save others, so you must also be able to save yourself. The verb here is in the second person plural, a verb form that was used at times by these Yiddish-speaking rebbes as a form of respect, as is found in many European languages (for example, German, where *Sie* would be both the plural and the respectful form). In Hebrew, even though there is no formal form for the pronoun "you," the author of the story has nonetheless inserted it into the language.

9   The rebbe is still ministering to his disciple, helping him in the process of letting go, and gently guiding him to understand that in his death he cannot necessarily focus on the needs of the living. This is good to remember when caring for someone nearing death—that while we may need to express our emotional needs, we also need to allow them to focus on their needs at this critical time.

〰   **He drew out greatly the word "tens of thousands" …** He lingered on these words as he saw a powerful, perhaps nearly overwhelming vision of all the people. With his intense empathy and caring, this gentle soul had already begun making the transition from this world to the next—from caring for those surrounding him on earth to the tens of thousands who needed him in the world-to-come.

10   The common practice before burial.

And he continued with this discourse until he came out of it and began to reveal wonderful teachings. And then he spoke of wonders—of what had happened to him—from then[7] until the fourth day of Sukkot, which was the day of his departure. There is not enough paper to write down all the wonderful things that happened in the last two months of his life, but we will tell some of it.

On Friday, on the [eve of the] holy Shabbat, before his departure, he was very weak and he was vomiting much blood and had almost expired, and his students stood before him. His principle disciple, R. Nathan, pleaded, "Rabbi, please save yourself."[8]

He answered, "I have no desire." He responded and said, "Rabbi, have compassion for your offspring and for your people." And he tilted his hand and said, "Slow down," as if he were saying I am already very far from this.[9]

Afterward he told a story from the Ba'al Shem Tov, who came to a place where there were great souls that he had to redeem, but he saw that the only way to repair them would have been by his own death. And he said, "For so long—so long—they have been waiting for me to come here. What can I say to you? 'Thousands [of them], thousands, tens of thousands, hundreds of thousands!'"

He drew out greatly the word "tens of thousands," meaning that there were in Uman tens of thousands of souls who were now standing around [waiting for him] to repair them, and because of this he suffered greatly.

On the last night of his life he returned and spoke on the subject of the souls. Afterward he instructed his students that as soon as he departed, while his body was still lying on the ground,[10] they take all of his writings that they would find in the closet and

(continued on page 57)

〰 **incinerate all of them ...** It is known that not all of his writings were burned, but how do we understand this desire for destruction? It can be important to ask yourself what you want to leave behind and to think about your legacy— to consider what is temporal, like journals that might contain hurtful information, and what will be lasting for those we leave behind. Passing on writing here appears to be also a way of showing love for his students. Communicating a deep appreciation of a friend can fulfill the words "Love is as strong as death" (Song of Songs 8:6), helping the dying person and the living feel deep connection that is a consolation for impending loss.

11 This instruction to incinerate his writings is one of many stories about the possible destruction of a rebbe's writings. In one about the Ba'al Shem Tov, he and his daughter Hodel were caught in a storm at sea while traveling to Israel with his beadle, R. Hirsch Sofer. The Besht said the storm was a sign from above either against his writings, that their contents not be revealed, or against his daughter, Hodel. Hodel said that she was ready to give her life in order to save her father's writings, and so she was lowered down to the water. But at the last minute she signaled that she should be pulled back up and told her father that it would be better if he were to throw his writings into the sea, because one day she would have a grandson who would write works even more eloquent than those of her father. That grandson was R. Nachman of Breslov.

Among Nachman's hidden works that were believed to have been destroyed were *Sefer haGanuz* ("The Scroll of Secrets," which only recently came to light and was translated) and *Sefer haNisraf* ("The Burned Book"). He told his disciples that both books contained deep mystical teachings that were not for the unschooled. Thus, though he dictated *Sefer haNisraf* to R. Nathan, Nathan said that he didn't understand it at all. "What I do remember," he said, "is that it spoke about the greatness of the mitzvah of hospitality and preparing the bed for a guest." The story goes that Nachman first had *Sefer haNisraf* destroyed two years before his death in a "bargain" for his life when he was suffering from tuberculosis, when he came to believe that the disease was punishment from God for having written the book in the first place.

12 The *etrog* is a fruit similar to a lemon but more aromatic and is one of four fruits and trees of the Land of Israel mentioned in the Torah as part of the celebration of the holiday of Sukkot; the biblical reference is to the *p'ri etz hadar*, literally, the "fruit of the beautiful [or splendid] tree" (Leviticus 23:40). The other three are the *lulav* (a closed date palm frond), the *hadas* (myrtle), and the *aravah* (willow), which collectively are referred to as a *lulav*.

incinerate all of them, and he warned them to fulfill his words.[11]
And they stood in a state both of alarm and sorrow, and they were
whispering to each other that he was already preparing himself to
depart. He said to them, "It's possible that you are speaking about
yourselves. What do you have to worry about when I am going
before you? Surely if those souls who did not know me at all are
waiting for me to redeem *them*, all the more so you [who are my
students] have nothing to fear at all."

In the morning he wrapped himself in his tallit [prayer shawl],
prayed and took the *etrog* and the *lulav*,[12] and finished the morning

(continued on page 59)

[~] **the Ari's siddur across his lap ...** In the face of illness and closeness to death, prayer and ritual can continue to provide structure and comfort for those for whom they have been meaningful. Even people with advanced dementia can sometimes be calmed and maybe even show joy when presented with deeply familiar practices.

[13] Arthur Green's translation of this story suggests that they were reading from the *Ma'avor Yavok*, a book published around 1626 in Mantua, Italy, written by Aaron Berechiah ben Moses of Modena. The book is about laws and customs related to sickness, deathbed, burial, and mourning rites. Ben Moses composed the work, according to his introduction, because many Jews in Mantua, and presumably throughout Italy, were remiss in "the great commandment of taking care of the dead." "I recently overheard," he writes, "that the community desired that one of its members undertake the task of arranging for them a prayer book so that they could join in song and prayer at the time of the going out of the soul." Thus, he continues, "I composed new ideas and different explanations to provide them as an offering and as incense in love and in reverence before the holy congregations" (Moss, 8).

[14] R. Nachman named no spiritual successor, and to this day, more than two hundred years after his death, he remains the sole spiritual leader of the Breslover Hasidim.

Hallel in a loud voice with **the Ari's siddur** [prayer book] **across his lap**. Afterward he instructed them to dress him nicely and to bathe him. And he took a circle of wax and rolled it between his fingers, thinking his awesome thoughts as the greats do—those whom, when they pondered such a subject, rolled wax and the like between their fingers. And even in the last hour [of his life] he was busy with supernal thoughts, with wondrous freedom, and with a clarity the likes of which has never been seen.

And when they saw that he was drawing near to the end, they began to recite over him the verses that are recited at the time of the departure of the *tzaddikim*.[13] And when it seemed that he had expired, they began to cry and shout out, "Our rabbi, our rabbi, to whom do you leave us?"[14]

(continued on page 61)

≈ **"I am not leaving you"** ... These words are preceded by the words, "as if to say." He didn't say these words, but it is what those surrounding him *felt* he said. The dying do leave their loved ones insofar as they are no longer physically or emotionally present, and there is a very real absence. However, the memory of them, a sense of their voice and closeness in our lives, their teachings, their actions, the shared experiences—both good and bad—all stay with the us long, long after a death. This is an important reminder that life is bigger and more amorphous than is easily explained, and we are bonded to one another in ways we may never entirely understand.

15 Abraham, Ishmael and Isaac, Jacob, and Aaron and Moses were each "gathered to his people" at the end of life, as depicted in the Torah.

≈ **He was released on the eighteenth of Tishrei** ... In the story of R. Nachman's death, his weakness is described as being present once he had settled in Uman. His Hasidim gathered around him on the Sabbath after Tisha b'Av, a time of comfort as we edge out of the deepest sadness of revisiting the destruction of the First and Second Temples. He died on the fourth day of the holiday of Sukkot (the eighteenth of the Hebrew month of Tishrei), in the very midst of a holiday that is about joy and on which we are commanded to be joyful. These are the bookends for his final weeks. Even though there is a depiction of the rabbi's suffering and vomiting of blood, we still have the sense that he achieved a very joyful journey for his soul as it continued up, higher on the ladder.

≈ See Insight Sparks: Cemeteries; Confession/*Vidui*; Clinging to God; Depression and Sadness; The End of Desire; Liminality; Talking with God.

And he opened his eyes and raised his head and his awesome face as if to say, **"I am not leaving you,"** and he expired and was gathered to his people[15] in holiness and purity.

He was released on the eighteenth of Tishrei, 5571 (October 16, 1810).

Cemeteries

Avraham "the Angel" asked for me, to be his neighbor in the cemetery, and I cannot refuse him. Therefore, I am informing you that I will shortly close up my days here and you will bury me next to his grave.

—From the deathbed story of R. Israel of Polotzk

Jewish custom requires burial of the body within twenty-four hours of the death and traces the roots of that custom back to biblical times. Rabbinic legend states that Adam and Eve learned about physical burial from a raven who showed them what to do with the body of their dead son, Abel (*Pirkei d'Rabbi Eliezer* 21). In Genesis 23, we read the story of the lengths to which Abraham went in order to secure a legal burying place for his wife Sarah, as well as for generations to follow. And in Exodus 13:19 we have the story of one of Moses's last acts in Egypt being the retrieval of Joseph's remains from the Nile in order to bury it in the Promised Land.

Repeatedly in Kings and Chronicles we have stories of dying people "sleeping with their ancestors" or being "gathered to their kin" (see "R. Nachman of Breslov" and "R. Avrahamli of Sochaczow"), in a concrete way evoking the role of community cemeteries.

Many Jews today choose to be buried in Jewish cemeteries, thus realizing the desire to remain connected to family or community even after death: "Bury me with my ancestors" was Jacob's request (Genesis 49:29) and the practice of most Jews today. However, geographic freedom and the dispersion of extended families away from one central home location are factors in a changing relationship to burial practices also marked by a rising rate of cremation among Jews. Visiting ancestral or parental graves today is not a common part of Jewish life, and yet it was once a central feature of Jewish practice. Cemeteries once housed burial associations and societies and small chapels and were an important facet of community. It is not so today. Outside of Israel, norms have shifted for most Jews. Even for those who do return to cemeteries in communities where they once lived, it is an infrequent pilgrimage and observed mitzvah.

What are the replacements? Cremation has become for many a valid alternative, as it can offer many people an alternative way to connect to earth and nature when ashes are scatted in a loved one's favorite place. And perhaps visits to Holocaust memorials, trips to family sites in Europe and Israel, and memorial plaques allow for more communal memory. However, nothing truly replaces the quiet, still nature and peace of a grave surrounded by the graves of other beloved family members.

We are losing the sense of a cemetery (in Hebrew, *beit kever*, "house of graves") as a house for those who have lived and loved together in life, a place where we can better imagine being gathered to our ancestors. How do we interpret for today Avraham the Angel's call from the grave asking R. Israel of Polotzk to be his neighbor in the cemetery, as quoted above? It is a call to find peace in burial side-by-side with a beloved friend. Is a physical resting place still of importance? If yes, do you have a family graveyard for burial and also possibly of ashes if cremation is preferred by some? These are important issues for a family to discuss and about which to try and reach agreement.

1 There are very few women described or quoted in the Hasidic literature, so it is interesting to note that Shneur Zalman has a well-documented relationship with his daughters. Of Shneur Zalman's daughter Freida, the Chabad chronicler Samuel Heilman writes, "She was very beloved by our Rebbe [R. Shneur Zalman] and he would say Hasidic discourses for her. When her brother the Mitteler Rebbe wanted to hear some specific topic from our Rebbe, he [i.e., her brother] would request from her that she should ask our Rebbe about this topic, and he [the rebbe] would tell her. Her brother used to hide in his [the rebbe's] room and listen" (Kaminetzy, 8). R. Shneur Zalman's relationship with his second daughter, Devorah Leah, evokes a similar self-sacrificing theme as the Ba'al Shem Tov's daughter Hodel. Devorah Leah is said to have given her life for her father in a mystical transaction enabling him to live on.

2 Translated as "Master of the *Tanya*," this is one of the names by which Shneur Zalman, the author of the *Tanya*, is known. The *Tanya* provides the interpretation and method of the Chabad approach to Hasidic mysticism.

3 This is one of Shneur Zalman's most important teachings, which is recorded in Menachem Mendel Schneerson's *Igrois Koidesh*. It is particularly remembered by Hasidim as the last thing he wrote. "For the truly humble soul, its mission in life lies in the pragmatic aspect of Torah, both in studying it for oneself and explaining it to others, and in doing acts of material kindness.... For although the divine attribute of Truth argued that man should not be created, since he is full of lies, the divine attribute of Kindness argued that he should be created, for he is full of kindnesses.... And the world is built upon kindness." In the face of death, R. Shneur Zalman affirms the purpose of Creation and the great importance of kindness, even over truth. This speaks deeply to the experience of nearing death, because caring for a person at the time of death and for the body after death is considered among the greatest acts of kindness. This final teaching establishes a level of holiness surrounding his death and affirms his legacy as one that emphasizes all that is good in humanity.

R. Shneur Zalman of Liadi

Shneur Zalman of Liadi (1745–1812) was an exceptional child, who, by the time he was eight years old, had written a full commentary on the Torah, including comments on the commentaries of Rashi, Nachmanides, and Abraham ibn Ezra. He was a student of the Maggid of Mezritch (see "R. DovBaer of Mezritch") and later of Menachem Mendel of Vitebsk. He was the author of many works but is best known for the *Tanya* (1796), the main work of the Chabad philosophy and its approach to Hasidic mysticism. The *Tanya*, which is also known by its formal title, *Likutei Amarim*, addresses Jewish spirituality, psychology, and theology, relating them to the study and practice of Kabbalah. The *Tanya* presents thoughts on how each person can serve God in his or her daily life. Shneur Zalman became the founder and first rebbe of Chabad Hasidism.[1]

R. Shneur Zalman of Liadi, the Ba'al haTanya,[2] on Saturday evening after *Havdalah* [the ritual marking the end of the Sabbath], a few moments before he gave his soul to eternal life, took a pen and wrote the teaching "The Truly Humble Soul,"[3] a teaching of great depth.

Afterward he asked one of his grandchildren, "Do you see the beam [in the ceiling]?"

(continued on page 67)

[4] In another version of this story, R. Shneur Zalman asks his grandson what he sees and his grandson replies, "'I see the cabin, the wooden wall, the beam in the ceiling.' R. Shneur Zalman answered him, 'And at the moment, I only see divinity.'" What seems to be happening is that Zalman is looking toward the heavens as he anticipates death and is seeing eternal life in unity with God, while his grandson sees only the material world.

〰 **all I see is the Divine Force …** It can be very disconcerting to the living to witness a person disengaging from life and possibly, like R. Shneur Zalman, entering a new reality. We achieve this with intentionality at times when we meditate on a natural scene or a beautiful phrase, run a marathon, or climb a mountain and we find ourselves lifted outside of a normal state into a greater consciousness. At the time of death it can seem like people sometimes simply are lifted up into an altered state, into the landscape or the mountains, or the line of poetry, or deep into their own world, and no longer have an attachment to the physical world and to us—and then it is up to us to also let go and trust that they are on their way to a place we do not yet know, the limitless realm of the *Ein Sof*, or living on in those who have been touched by them.

[5] This is the first death presented in these stories where "great joy" is introduced. We will see it again in the deaths of Shneur Zalman's disciple, R. Aaron of Staroselye.

[6] This phrase is a quote from the beginning of the *Idra Zuta* describing the death of R. Shimon bar Yochai (first century CE), a preeminent student of R. Akiva and purported worker of miracles. Many kabbalists attribute authorship of the *Zohar* to him, though historically the author is known to be Moses de León, a thirteenth-century Spanish kabbalist (see *Idra Zuta* on *Zohar*, part III, 287a).

[7] *Ein Sof* ("Without End") is one of the many names for God and in Kabbalah is understood to be the un-boundaried, limitless God who exists without form before Creation took place. When R. Shneur Zalman dies, he joins God in a state that is before Creation, formless and unending.

〰 See Insight Sparks: Clinging to God; Unification.

And his grandson was surprised and didn't know how to respond.[4] So R. Zalman said to his grandson, "Believe me that I do not see [it either]; **all I see is the Divine Force**, which enlivens everything material, and except for that, I do not see anything."

Afterward he spoke further words of Torah with great joy[5] and a wondrous conjoining [with God] until all those standing around him were astonished and amazed. And then "he gathered his feet on to the bed" and tied himself into a single bundle[6] with the *Ein Sof*.[7]

He was released on the twenty-fourth of Tevet, 5573 (December 27, 1812).

1 This is a name of R. Shneur Zalman of Liadi.

〜 **joyful and of good heart ...** In this death and in the death of his father and brother we see pure joy and goodness. In the introduction to *The Book of Departure*, Mintz says, "For them [the *tzaddikim*] the day of death is turned into a day of celebration," because their souls are about to be reunified with God. In the stories of generations here, we see the power of a positive experience created by the father on his deathbed, helped by a supportive teaching from the tradition informing the experience of death for the children who follow. Death is again peaceful and uplifting, and not full of fear or loneliness. While we may not ourselves envision joy in death, we can hope to achieve a sense of peace, unity with those we love, and gratitude for a life well lived.

2 The word *chesed* is often translated as "loving-kindness" and is one of the ten attributes of God in Kabbalah. It is through the emanations of these attributes that God is revealed and through which God continuously creates both the physical realm and the chain of higher metaphysical realms. The sense of the expression here is that one could see God's kindness emanating like a thread of gold wrapped around R. DovBaer's face. This expression is used also in the Talmud to describe God's loving presence: "Resh Lakish says: To him who is engaged in the study of the Torah by night, the Holy One extends a thread of *chesed* by day, as it is said, 'By day Adonai will command God's loving-kindness, and in the night God's song shall be with me' (Psalm 42:9)" (Talmud, *Avodah Zarah* 3b).

3 Psalm 31:6. The full verse says, "I shall entrust my spirit in Your hand; You redeemed me, O Adonai, God of Truth."

R. DovBaer,
Son of the Ba'al haTanya

Upon the death of his father, Shneur Zalman of Liadi, R. DovBaer (1773–1835) assumed the role of the second rebbe of Chabad Hasidism and moved to the town of Lubavitchi, the name of which eventually became an integral part of the movement's name (Lubavitch Hasidim). His position was disputed by one of his father's students, R. Aaron of Staroselye, who founded an alternative yeshivah, which differed from DovBaer's regarding the emphasis on and correct method of emotional expression in Hasidic prayer. DovBaer's son-in-law, R. Menachem Mendel of Lubavitch, eventually headed the yeshivah and later became his successor.

Some days before his departure, R. DovBaer, son of the Ba'al haTanya[1] was **joyful and of good heart**—"a thread of Divine *chesed*[2] was drawn about his face." They constantly heard from his mouth the phrase "I shall entrust my spirit in Your hand."[3]

(continued on page 71)

4   Psalm 36:10.

5   The same was said of R. Shimon bar Yochai (see "R. Menachem Mendel of Riminov," note 6).

6   This is the second half of the verse just quoted; thus, "With You is the fountain of life; by Your light do we see light."

∿ **entrusted his soul with the highest heavens ...** God's light illuminates the world for him, and he is able to be in a state of joy as he teaches his final lessons to his students and can entrust his soul to God. Belief and trust in something can be very powerful for those who feel it with the entirety of their being. R. DovBaer dies wholly at peace and in a state of quiet joyful ecstasy.

∿ See Insight Sparks: Clinging to God; The Timing of Death; Unification.

Two hours before his departure, he began to expound on the verse "For with You is the source of life."[4] And many of his most committed Hasidim were there, and they said that they had never heard such hidden secrets from him.[5] And the explanation continued for about two hours, until he came to explain the verse "by Your light do we see light,"[6] and with these words he became silent and **entrusted his soul with the highest heavens**.

He was released in 5595 (1835).

The Timing of Death

"Death would be better for me than such a life. God of truth, take my soul!" God heard his prayer and raised his soul to the high heavens.

—From the deathbed story of R. Rafael of Bershad

The biblical model of powerlessness in relation to the time of death is Moses, who died before entering the Promised Land of Israel. This remains our guiding paradigm for having to accept that life is about the journey rather than reaching our biggest goals. Generations of Jews lived without the possibility of arriving in Israel but took a few steps perhaps on the journey and were comforted by Moses's example of greatness that stops before the final goal has been met.

Many of the rebbes in the stories in *The Book of Departure* seem to have significant agency in the timing of their deaths, dying on a holiday or seemingly having God take their soul by their will, as with R. Rafael of Bershad. Others show their agency by enacting a specific action just prior to the moment they die: "And he said, 'Good night,' and he slept [i.e., he died]" (see "R. DovBaer of Mezritch"); "Immediately, when he was done speaking his words, he gathered his feet into the bed, closed his eyes, and conveyed his holy soul to the God of the spirits" (see "R. Israel of Polotzk"). There is a sense of intentionality in these stories—as if the rabbis could control the moment or the day on which they died. Many people seem to hold on to life in order to live until a significant event: the arrival of someone who lives far away, an important birthday, a wedding, or a birth in the family.

While we can't ensure the timing of death, the quality of the time leading up to death is something that we can influence and change. We can with effort ensure that a person's wishes will be followed, that the honey is indeed brought in a big saucer and he doesn't say, "One has no authority on the day of death" (the Ba'al Shem Tov)—and that a person's voice is made strong even at a time of profound weakness and continued loss of strength. It is the final expression of *kavod*, of honor, when we continue to hear and abide by a person's voice even as his or her strength wanes.

In two of the stories the *tzaddikim* are possibly choosing to die sooner, sending the doctor away and refusing medication: R. Menachem Mendel of Kotzk and R. Yekutiel Yehudah, saying that his work is done in this world. People often struggle with when to stop attempting curative measures in the face of terminal and often insufferable illness. These are extremely difficult and very personal decisions; there is no one right answer.

Some guidance and permission to allow for death in situations when a person is close to dying are found in the Talmudic story (*Ketubot* 104a) of how R. Yehudah haNasi's handmaid, Kallah, stopped others from praying to allow her rabbi to die:

> Rabbi [Yehudah haNasi]'s handmaid went up to the roof and prayed, "Those above [i.e., the immortals or the angels] desire Rabbi to join them, and those below [i.e., the mortals] desire Rabbi to stay with them. May it be God's will that the mortals may overpower the immortals." However, once she saw how many times he got up to go to the privy, removing his tefillin and putting them on again, she regretted what she had said and prayed, "May it be God's will that the immortals may overpower the mortals." But the Rabbis were not silent in their prayers for heavenly mercy, so Kallah threw a jar from the roof to the ground. And for a moment they were silent—and the soul of Rabbi departed to its eternal rest.

Whether people are holding on to life and trying to live another day, or making decisions to take away medications or interventions in order for life to end so they can be spared further suffering, we must understand that they are not *tzaddikim* who could often determine the day of death. Rather, they are ordinary people who have *no* say in the timing of death and, in the case of illness and old age, possibly struggle a very long time until the release of death arrives.

1 Literally, "deputy," or the one who fills his place, hence, his *successor* or *stand-in*.

2 On Hoshanah Rabbah there is a lot of joyful celebration and then one takes the willow leaves from the *lulav* and smashes them repeatedly on the ground—showing that R. Aaron was at this point still strong and seemingly healthy.

〜 **At night he went to the *hakafot* ...** We're given a model here of a rabbi who is living life fully and with spirit right up until the moment of death—a model for us and those we love as we approach death, to live each day fully.

3 *Hakafot* means "circuits" and describes a part of the prayer services on Sukkot and Simchat Torah when people walk or dance around in a circle. On the festival of Sukkot people walk in a circle carrying their *lulav* and *etrog* and making blessings. On Simchat Torah people generally walk or dance with singing and spirit around the perimeter of the synagogue with some people in the middle dancing with the Torah scrolls. Circle dancing is very common in Hasidic celebrations today and can be an almost ecstatic practice, with loud singing or band music and the pace becoming frenzied at times. The circle in many traditions represents unity, perfection, and community and is a concept very close to the hearts of Hasidim.

4 R. Aaron chooses a verse that describes Solomon sending all the celebrants home after the dedication of the Temple joyful and full of a sense of God's goodness (1 Kings 8:66). Here it is also the end of the holiday on which historically people made a pilgrimage to the Temple and then returned home. As this verse is R. Aaron's last teaching, the story communicates a sense of fulfillment of what God has commanded, closeness to God, and completion before the unexpected end of the rebbe's life.

R. Aaron of Staroselye

R. Aaron of Staroselye (ca. 1766–1832) was one of the strongest disciples of Shneur Zalman of Liadi (the Ba'al haTanya) and contended with Shneur Zalman's son DovBaer (see "R. DovBaer, Son of the Ba'al haTanya") as his legitimate successor. His emphasis was on the importance of emotion in prayer, which is where he and DovBaer disagreed. DovBaer believed that emotion in prayer can only be a result of contemplation (*hitbonenut*), while R. Aaron believed in the emotion itself. It was he who urged Shneur Zalman to publish his great work the *Tanya*.

R. Aaron of Staroselye, the successor[1] of the Ba'al haTanya, departed on the night of Shemini Atzeret.

On the day of Hoshanah Rabbah[2] he prayed as he always did—he jumped, skipped, and danced at the time of his prayer, for he was then completely healthy. And he finished his prayer at four in the afternoon and broke the *lulav* to bits. **At night he went to the hakafot.**[3]

After the *hakafot* he lay down on his bed and began to say a teaching on the verse "On the eighth day he sent the people away."[4]

(continued on page 77)

⟿ **in the middle of the teaching ...** He died in the midst of an active life in community. This can feel tragic for the community and for the people close to a person even when a person has led a long and full life, for they have little warning of the impending loss. This story finds meaning in R. Aaron's final teaching and in the timing of his death at the end of a joyous holiday, to try and make peace. It can be important to reflect on the fullness of a person's life so as not to only dwell in the emptiness of the loss.

⟿ **twenty-fifth of Tishrei ...** In 1832, the twenty-fifth of the Hebrew month Tishrei, the day R. Aaron died, was a Thursday, the day on which the annual cycle of reading the Torah would have begun with the first reading from Genesis. Though not a holiday, this was still a special day in the Jewish year and provided his followers with a sense that there was intentionality to his death on that day.

⟿ See Insight Sparks: Purity; The Timing of Death.

And **in the middle of the teaching** he told R. Avraham Shinas to complete the teaching, and then he left life to the living and gave his soul in purity.

He was released on the **twenty-fifth of Tishrei**, 5593 (October 19, 1832).

[1] This is the first mention of an event in world history in any of these stories. The Napoleonic Empire was at its peak in Europe in 1810. In June 1812, Napoleon attacked Russia with a force of 650,000 soldiers; he left in December of that year. Whatever the outcome of this war, the rebbe viewed this great war as the Apocalypse, what the book of Daniel calls the "end of days" (12:13), after which time the Messiah would come.

[2] The *Machshevei Katzin* (the "Calculators of the End") was a group of Hasidim who focused on figuring out the day on which the Messiah would come.

[3] On Passover the four cups of wine drunk at the seder represent *bringing* Israel out of Egypt, *deliverance* from slavery, *redemption*, and God *taking* Israel to be God's people. There is no formal "Cup of Salvation" at the seder, though it may be referring to the second cup, or it is likely that he is raising the Cup of Elijah, which is associated with the coming of the Messiah.

[4] "Scattered" can also be translated as "the bond was snapped" (Talmud, *Avodah Zarah* 10b). In the Talmudic text, this phrase implies death: "When Antoninus died, Rabbi exclaimed, 'The bond is snapped!' [So also] when Artaban died, Rav exclaimed, 'The bond is snapped!'" Since the Hasidim never say that a rebbe has "died" (rather, they use more obtuse language), by using this expression, the story is making clear that everyone but R. Menachem Mendel of Riminov had died.

R. Menachem Mendel
of Riminov

Menachem Mendel of Riminov (1745–1815) was introduced to Hasidism as a young boy, when he met R. DovBaer of Mezritch. He eventually became a disciple of R. Elimelech of Lizhensk and was an important Hasidic leader in Poland. He is known for his asceticism and mystical support for Napoleon, whose wars he identified with the battles of Gog and Magog and the advent of the messianic age.

In the year 5573 [1813], the land trembled from the war between Napoleon and Russia,[1] and Those Who Calculate the End of Days[2] found that the time was ripe for complete redemption. R. Menachem Mendel said, "Petition God on my behalf so that He will lengthen my days until after the year 5575 [1815] has passed, then you will be certain that you will be privileged to hear the shofar of the Messiah."

On the night of Passover at the time of the seder he said, "If they will support me, we will merit the coming of the Messiah this year."

And when he lifted the cup [at the seder], he said that this is the Cup of Salvation[3] for the whole of Israel—if only all the *tzaddikim* of the generation would agree with him.

The Maggid of Koznitz had departed because of the sins of the generation on Erev Sukkot, and all vision was hidden from the Seer of Lublin, and the group was scattered,[4] and only R. Mendel of Riminov remained.

From Shemini Atzeret until Hanukkah in the year 5575 he would do *hakafot* every night with a minyan of those close to him. After Passover his health slackened and his strength weakened

(continued on page 81)

〰 **"Oy, the whole world is passing from me!"** ... At the beginning of this story we hear from Menachem Mendel that if he can live through the next year, and if he has the support of all the people and the agreement of all the *tzaddikim*, he will—or his death will—precipitate the coming of the Messiah. Now with his imminent death, which he foresees, he announces that the Messiah's coming is once again far away. He is recognizing his loss of ability to contribute to the salvation of the world. A parallel experience today is perhaps the way that giving up their work when it has been central and meaningful in their life can leave many people feeling a sense of tremendous sadness in their inability to continue making a difference in the greater world.

5 In this book we will use this Hebrew term, *goses*, for a dying person in the last days of life; it quite specifically means in rabbinic literature what today's medical professionals would refer to as a state of "actively dying" (see the appendix, "The Characteristics of Active Dying"), wherein a person has no more than a few days, hours, or only minutes to live.

〰 **Copperhead snakes ...** The snakes mentioned here are related to the pit viper and are one of the most venomous and dangerous snakes. They are distinctive for their copper color, prow-shaped heads, and green wormlike tails when young. Thus, Menachem Mendel refers to them as "green worms with copper beaks." This description of the copper color of this venomous snake also provides insight into the story of Moses where he creates a staff with a copper serpent mounted on it to cure the plague of serpents that threatens the Israelites: "The people came to Moses and said, 'We sinned by speaking against Adonai and against you. Intercede with Adonai to take away the serpents from us!' And Moses interceded for the people. Then Adonai said to Moses, 'Make a seraph [i.e., a serpent] figure and mount it on a standard. And if anyone who is bitten looks at it, he shall recover.' Moses made a copper serpent and mounted it on a standard; and when anyone was bitten by a serpent, he would look at the copper serpent and recover" (Numbers 21:7–9). Finally, it is interesting to note that the Hebrew word for "serpent," *nachash*, is quite closely related to the word for "copper," *nachoshet*.

The Israelites needed Moses and his copper-headed staff to save the people and lead them forward, and Menachem Mendel is telling his followers that he is unable to provide any such salvation.

until Lag b'Omer. On that day he purified and sanctified himself, and sat in his chair and said, **"Oy, the whole world is passing from me!"**

R. Naftali of Ropshitz, who was present, wept bitterly and said, "Reveal for us, Rabbeinu, when the end will be." Then, the *goses*[5] opened his eyes and said, **"Copperhead snakes** will crawl over you before the Messiah comes."

(continued on page 83)

⟿ **return until the next day ...** The return of Menachem Mendel's soul signals that the united prayers of the people still do have some power and can give them some hope in the face of loss. However, if he had died that day, on Lag b'Omer, it would have signaled a greater message of reunification, given that it is the day of weddings and covenant. The fact that the departure of his soul was postponed a day is consistent with this story of unfulfilled messianic hope.

6 The time of the Counting of the Omer, the days between Passover and Shavuot (the day celebrating the giving of Torah) is a time of partial mourning. The observance of the thirty-third day of Counting the Omer (Lag b'Omer), the *only* day of the forty-nine days of the counting when one can celebrate, get married, and so on, is a day of bonfires and great merriment. It also marks the anniversary of the death of R. Shimon bar Yochai and the day on which he revealed the deepest secrets of Kabbalah in the form of the *Zohar*.

⟿ See Insight Spark: Dying on an Auspicious Day.

He was silent and his soul flew away, but the sound of the wailing of R. Naftali of Ropshitz and all those gathered caused his soul to **return until the next day**, the thirty-fourth day of the Counting of the Omer.[6]

He was released on the nineteenth of Iyar, 5575 (May 29, 1815).

Dying on an Auspicious Day

The most deeply honored day of all days in the opinion of the Sages is the day of death—even more important than the day of birth.

—Benjamin Mintz, introduction to *The Book of Departure*

In his introduction to *The Book of Departure*, Benjamin Mintz explains that the day of death would be cause for rejoicing. Also, dying on a Shabbat or holiday is traditionally thought to be a sign of additional blessing for the deceased and is viewed as helping the bereaved through their loss by adding this special gloss.

Nonetheless, loss is painful, and many who have lost a loved one on a holiday feel that the holiday will be ruined forever, and the joy of the holiday is also lost. So, while the day may indeed be an auspicious one, a loved one's death on a holiday may only serve to complicate our bereavement all the more.

How do we reconcile these disparate emotions? How do we help ourselves or others through bereavement when a loved one has died on a holiday, leaving us feeling that the holiday is now "ruined"? What is the idea behind this notion of the day of death being possibly a day of celebration? With birth, all of life and its possibilities lie in front of a person, and much is unknown. However, with death, we can be witness to all the good that people have done in their lives, the impact they have had, and we can experience gratitude for what they gave us.

Perhaps considering ways in which the holiday may be actually *enhanced* through this new *yahrzeit* can help; a holiday is now possibly made all the more important to a family *because* Grandma/Bubbe died on that day, and we can bring her into our annual celebration by remembering her and all that she gave to us.

Within the traditional teaching for Shavuot—the day on which the Ba'al Shem Tov died—Exodus 19:3–4 teaches that "Moses ascended to God, and Adonai called to him from the mountain, saying, 'So shall you say to the house of Jacob and tell the children of Israel: You have seen what I did to the Egyptians, and [how] I bore you on eagles' wings, *and I brought you to Me.*'" This teaches that when people die it is not a simple matter of being no more, and not even that they have "gone to God." No, it is much more than that: God has *brought them* into God's Divine Presence—or, stated another way, they have arrived at a place of wholeness and peace, perhaps also a comforting reminder for people as the holiday/*yahrzeit* approaches.

〰 **to bring the people back to Judaism ...** The organized North American Jewish communities in the last forty years have focused a good deal of effort on the problems associated with assimilation and dispersion, and it seems like rabbis of the seventeenth to nineteenth centuries had to deal with similar challenges.

1 The *chevra kadisha*, or burial society (literally, "holy society"), is made up of community volunteers who generally remain anonymous for the sake of modesty and respect for the deceased and do the traditional washing, dressing, and blessing of the body of the deceased.

〰 **asked for me ...** When two people have shared a meaningful relationship, there can be a sense of being drawn to one's beloved or dear friend. This "call" from one who has departed can be salve to a broken heart and might also be a logical way that a person experiences life after the loss of deep companionship. The only emotional path available might be to feel the pull to join the other in death. This story can help us understand the emotional and spiritual longing sometimes experienced by some bereaved people when a broken heart might lead them to wish to join their beloved through their own death.

〰 **when he was done speaking ...** The story here echoes the story of Jacob in the Torah, "When Jacob finished his instructions to his sons, he drew his feet into the bed and, breathing his last, he was gathered to his people" (Genesis 49:33). There is a sense of completion; it's time, and the *tzaddik* in the tradition of Jacob accepts this holy moment.

〰 **conveyed his holy soul ...** This is an active verb; R. Israel does the conveying here, not God, not the Angel of Death. He is not *taken*, but he is able to *give up* his own soul. It can seem in some cases that people choose the moment of death and that there is a conscious moment of letting go.

〰 See Insight Spark: Cemeteries.

R. Israel (ben Perez) of Polotzk

R. Israel of Polotzk (d. ca. 1785) was among the leading disciples of R. DovBaer of Mezritch. In 1777, he moved to the Land of Israel along with R. Menachem Mendel of Vitebsk and a significant number of other Hasidim and settled in Safed. He was an important preacher, recruiter, and fund-raiser for the Hasidic movement. His teachings very much focused on repentance.

It was the custom of R. Israel of Polotzk to travel through the countryside in order **to bring the people back to Judaism**. And so, when he crossed through to the town of Kavostov, where R. Avraham "the Angel" was buried, he went to pray at the holy grave. When he returned to the inn, he lay on his bed and sent for the *chevra kadisha*[1] and said to them, "Avraham 'the Angel' **asked for me**, to be his neighbor in the cemetery, and I cannot refuse him. Therefore, I am informing you that I will shortly close up my days here and you will bury me next to his grave."

Immediately, **when he was done speaking** his words, he gathered his feet into the bed, closed his eyes, and **conveyed his holy soul** to the God of the spirits.

1   R. Yaakov Yitzchak Rabinowicz of Przysucha (1766–1813), also referred to as HaYehudi haKodesh, "the Holy Jew," a student of the Seer of Lublin.

2   A rabbinic way of saying that they came to consensus. (See Berger, 48–49.)

~   **to speed up and hurry the coming of the Messiah ...** As with the story of R. Menachem Mendel of Riminov, they did not succeed in bringing on or hurrying the coming of the Messiah, described also as the "time of the nightingale" (see below). The background to the story is that the three *tzaddikim* in our story tried to force God to send the Messiah on Simchat Torah by bombarding heaven with their prayers. The heavens became angered, and so the Maggid of Koznitz died before Sukkot, the Jew from Przysucha (some say it was Menachem Mendel of Riminov) died six months later, and the Seer of Lublin shortly thereafter. They are thought to have been punished for trying to tell God what to do. What does "bringing the Messiah" mean to us today? Perhaps the parallel here is to the person who has not achieved a life goal, whatever that might be, and the disappointment that might be palpable in the person's relationship to the final weeks or days of life. At these times it could be that the best we can do is to reassure the person who is dying that we or someone else who has been influenced by that person will carry his or her torch further.

3   The "time of the nightingale" is a reference to Song of Songs (2:12), when the lover urges his maiden to run away with him as spring approaches, a hopeful and romantic metaphor for the coming of the Messiah. Here it seems the time of the Messiah does not appear to be coming any nearer even though two *tzaddikim* have now departed. Possibly, the Seer believes that his leap from the window might be enough to convince God to bring the Messiah.

~   R. Menachem seems to predict and possibly choose the day upon which he dies. What of those who decide that their lives are over and choose to stop living through refusing surgery, food and fluids, dialysis treatment, cancer treatment, or possibly attempting suicide? The Seer's death is preceded by his fall, which to this day is disputed as to whether it was a suicide attempt. This debate opens the door to questions like these: Are people who make decisions

The Seer of Lublin

Yaakov Yitzchak Horowitz (1745–1815), known as the *Chozeh* (Seer) of Lublin, was a leading figure in the early Hasidic movement and in its spread through Poland. He was nearly blind, yet he was called the "Seer" due to his reportedly intuitive powers. Horowitz was a disciple of the Maggid of Mezritch (see "R. DovBaer of Mezritch") and continued his studies under R. Elimelech of Lizhensk, who reportedly gave the Seer his vision. He gained a reputation as a miracle worker who could repair people's souls.

In the year 5574, the three fathers of the world, the Seer of Lublin, the Jew from Przysucha,[1] and the Maggid of Koznitz, voted and decided[2] **to speed up and hurry the coming of the Messiah**. It is known and has been made public what resulted from it, that all of them departed in one year—though for different and sundry reasons—for the time of the nightingale[3] had not yet come.

(continued on page 91)

that others see as going against their medical needs interfering with God's will or going against human morality and the doctor's oath to heal; or are they, like R. Menachem (whether it is suicide or giving up life), understanding some greater or highly personal truth that tells them that it is the right time for them to die?

How do we understand the rabbis' life commitment to the coming of the Messiah in today's world? Perhaps the lesson is one of hopefulness. In a world where it can feel as if humanity were descending rather than ascending, messianism is the belief that inch by inch we can do better. We will and can resolve the big issues of our time such as climate change, international hunger, terrorism, and racism. As much as it can feel that more knowledge is not bringing us closer to greater peace, we sustain faith in our capacity to do better.

4 A play on words here, using the Hebrew *nifla'ah*, "wondrous," which also relates to the Seer's *nefilah*, his "fall."

〜 **the awesome story of the "fall"** … On Simchat Torah, in the middle of the *hakafot* (the dancing around the room "in circles," carrying the Torah, that occurs on this joyous holiday), the Seer went into his room, where he suffered what his Hasidim termed a *nefilah*—literally, a "falling." While "falling" is often considered a metaphor for a disruption in our relationship with the Divine, here it is also a literal "fall," out of his window. He lay unconscious for a period of time and then fled the town. He was found by his anxious students sitting on a rock on the outskirts of the town in a black depression. He died almost a year later from injuries relating to the fall. Instead of the Messiah coming on Tisha b'Av as the three Rabbis had predicted and transforming the nature of the day from sadness to rejoicing, it became the day of his death, adding to the tragedies remembered on this day.

〜 **"… I would not give them even a spoonful of water."** … This expression reflects that fasting is suffering, while food and drink represent celebration. The death of a *tzaddik* is generally perceived as a joyous occasion by Hasidism, as the deceased becomes closer to God and in this way the rebbe's followers also become closer. However, rejoicing in death becomes a very different event when it becomes an occasion for enemies to celebrate the downfall of someone whose teachings they rejected.

5 Thus, he dies on Tisha b'Av, a day of complete fasting, when his opponents couldn't celebrate, not even with a spoonful of water.

Especially awesome and wonderful[4] was the departure of the Seer of Lublin:

On Simchat Torah of that year at the time of the *hakafot* there was **the awesome story of the "fall"** known to Hasidim, but concerning it they shared only veiled hints, softly spoken words with tremulous quaking.

And our rabbi then *fell* upon his deathbed [though not yet departed], and opponents of our master drank and rejoiced about this. And when the matter was known to him, he said, "They think that at the time of my departure they will drink and celebrate much more. They can be sure that **I would not give them even a spoonful of water.**"[5]

And so it was, because he ascended to the heavens on Tisha b'Av.

(continued on page 93)

6 This is an idiom meaning "he was about to die." The *Shulchan Aruch* uses this expression, translated here as "terminally ill," to convey imminent death: "It is prohibited to ask a non-Jew to travel outside of the *techum* [village boundaries] on Shabbat to notify the relatives of the deceased to come and to eulogize him. However, concerning a terminally ill person who asks that his relatives be notified it is definitely permitted" (*Shulchan Aruch, Orach Chayim* 306:9).

7 This is an expression of his intense loyalty that evokes the story of Joshua bin Nun and his loyalty to Moses in Exodus 33:11, "And he would then return to the camp, but his attendant, Joshua bin Nun, a youth, would not stir out of the tent."

8 The day that the Seer died is here described as the day on which the will of heaven overcame the wills of those on earth, the Hasidim of the Seer who wished and prayed to prolong his life. This expression links the story to the famous story in the Talmud (*Ketubot* 104a) of the death of the great Yehudah haNasi ("the Prince"), when similarly the heavens (the *aralim*) overcame the *tzaddikim* (the *metzukim*) on earth, resulting in his death. In that story, R. Yehudah's handmaid understood that his suffering was too much and it was time for him to die. She intentionally dropped and smashed a vessel from the roof, which so startled R. Yehudah's students that they momentarily stopped their prayers on his behalf, and in that very moment, his soul ascended. (This story is also evoked in the stories of R. Yechiel Michel of Zlotshov, R. Menachem Mendel of Vitebsk, and R. Shlomo, the *Kohen* of Radomsk, where the quote is slightly expanded to include describing R. Yehudah as "the holy ark.") This becomes an expression that describes those special situations when a group of people gather to pray in order to save someone when the person, however, has a medical condition that is terminal and progressing. It honors the prayers of those on earth by mentioning them as a force to be reckoned with and that need to be overcome for the person to die.

~ **endless sorrow is the day of Tisha b'Av ...** This is what we may experience when facing death, our own or someone's who is central in our lives, and all we see before us is the loss of everything we have known, believed, and loved. Thus, too, for this great leader of many, the students of the rebbe equate his death with the worst day in the history of Judaism, when hopes, dreams, Temples, and thousands of lives were lost.

9 With the death of their rebbe, they feel that their entire world has been destroyed, and thus they equate it to the day of Tisha b'Av, the day that memorializes the destruction of both the First and Second Temples.

When the event of "the falling" became well known among his students, they started flocking from all the communities. Only R. Naftali from Ropshitz was absent. After Purim, when his students saw that the world was "harsh to him,"[6] they sent a special representative to R. Naftali that he should come soon, and so it was that he [i.e., Naftali] came soon and he saw the suffering of the great scholar and the major confusion.

And from then on he never left the tent of his *rav*.[7] And during the twelve days from Rosh Hodesh Nisan until the thirteenth day when we read [from Torah] of the dedication of the altar, the twelve heads of the twelve tribes (which correspond to the twelve months of the year), he did not give sleep to his eyes nor leave the bed of the Seer. When the thirteenth day of Nisan arrived, as soon as the morning rose, R. Naftali turned and went to his lodging.

The remaining students of the Seer, the greats of Israel who remained in his house, sent for him [i.e., Naftali] every day that he should come, but he never took notice of them and he did whatever he was doing, but he didn't come until the "day of their bitterness" on which "the *aralim* were victorious over the *metzukim*"[8]—a fixed day of **endless sorrow is the day of Tisha b'Av.**[9] Also on that day they sent for him. And at noon R. Naftali left his inn and walked slowly to the Seer's house, and just as he stepped on the doorstep of the house, with a wondrous passion the soul of the Seer left him for *Hashem*, may He be blessed.

(continued on page 95)

10 In other words, Nisan, as established by Torah (Exodus 12:2 and Deuteronomy 16:1), was considered the first month of the year, and each of the days after the first of the month until the twelfth day corresponds to a different month, and traditionally to a different tribe as well, since each of the tribes in turn brought sacrifices during this period. Av, the fifth month, corresponds then to the fifth day of Nisan, offering a prediction on this basis that the Seer would die that day.

11 This quote from the Talmud (*Avodah Zarah* 20a) refers to the wife of Tineius Rufus, a tyrannical governor of Judea in the first century CE. The Talmudic story relates that when R. Akiva saw her "he spat, then laughed, and then wept. 'Spat' because of her originating from a mere putrefying drop [of semen]; 'laughed' because he foresaw that she would become a proselyte and that he would marry her; 'wept' that such beauty should [ultimately] whither in the dust." Naftali of Ropshitz evokes this story to express the intense sadness of losing someone even while accepting his or her humanity and to signal the dramatic incongruity between the life of a great person and the dust to which we all return.

~ **was released on Tisha b'Av ...** This death is not on Shabbat or on a joyful holiday, but on an important historic day of communal mourning. Perhaps dying on Tisha b'Av means that a great Hasidic dream was also dying, as the Messiah had not arrived according to human plans.

~ See Insight Sparks: Dying on an Auspicious Day; The Timing of Death.

And R. Naftali of Ropshitz himself explained how he knew when the Seer would die. It is known that the twelve days between Rosh Hodesh Nisan and the thirteenth [of Nisan] correspond to the twelve months of the year, and the Seer used to write every day during those days about what will happen in the corresponding month.[10] And on the fifth day of the month of Nisan that year corresponding to the month of Av, he said, "I only see the day of Tisha b'Av until noon."

And he understood what this alluded to. "Woe this beauty that withers in the dust."[11]

He **was released on Tisha b'Av** 5575 (August 15, 1815).

The Language of Death

For *tzaddikim,* we don't [use the term] "death" at all; [we only speak of] "a departure" from this lowly world and a rising up to the world-to-come. The soul departs from the body, the spirit from the material.

—Benjamin Mintz, introduction to *The Book of Departure*

The two key words for "death" in these texts are *histalkut* and *petirah* (as a verb, this word commonly appears as *niftar*). Both words can be translated either as "departure" or as "death"—the final departure—and by itself *petirah* has a wider range of meanings, including "to take leave," "to release," and "to dismiss." But since the introduction to *The Book of Departure* tells us that "for *tzaddikim,* we don't [use the term] 'death' at all," we have here heeded the author's warning and have tried not to use the English word "death" in translating either word. Rather, we have used "departure" for the word *histalkut* and "release" for the more passive verb form of the word *petirah.* There are specific instances where we translated *petirah* as "death," particularly when the text is specifically referring to death of the body in contrast to the soul.

It is worth noting the subtle differences between the "directionality" with which the words *histalkut* and *petirah* are used in the literature— evoking vertical and horizontal relationships. The Rabbis have a strong sense of God's place being "up"—in the heavens, or *bashamayim*—and of our earthly life as being "below," and so the preferred use of the Aramaic root *samech-lamed-kuf,* meaning "to ascend," when one speaks of the departure of the Rabbis.

The verb *niftar,* on the other hand, deriving from the verb *pei-tet-resh,* means "to break through" or "to open," as in "opening a womb," *petter rechem* in Hebrew, a woman's first birthed son. In its noun form it can mean an "exemption" (as in legal writings) or a "release," thus, a forward movement, or even death itself—a release from life.

Each of us may think of death in our own way: as an active or a passive process, as a moving "up" or a moving "out," as a death of the body separate from the ongoing life of the soul, or as absolute nothingness. However, it is not *our* concepts of death that are critical in bringing comfort to the dying, but our understanding of the way in which the dying person understands death and afterlife.

〰 **This is where I will rest forever ...** Thinking through all of one's end-of-life issues is a kindness done for family and loved ones by the person who will die so that one's end-of-life wishes are known and there is no need for guesswork. This often can take a burden off the family, if they have had a chance to understand and accept those choices and can be comfortable with the outcomes. This requires talking openly about dying, preparing detailed advance directives that are updated regularly, and directions for what is desired after death, including the choice of cremation or burial and how a person will be memorialized.

1 Psalm 132:14.

〰 See Insight Spark: Cemeteries; Ethical Wills and Advance Directives; The Timing of Death.

R. Eliezer haLevi Horowitz

R. Eliezer haLevi Horowitz (1740–1809) was a disciple of R. Elimelech of Lizhensk, the Seer of Lublin, and the Maggid of Koznitz. He served as rabbi in Tarnograd but died in Koznitz. He is remembered for his book *Noam Megadim*, a well-known text that follows the weekly Torah readings. According to one of his sayings, even the greatest saint has to hide his own light to avoid the sin of pride.

R. Eliezer haLevi Horowitz, author of the *Noam Megadim*, once traveled, as was his habit, from the Seer of Lublin to the Maggid of Koznitz. When he reached the outskirts of the city, he saw a graveyard from afar and said, "How nice is this place! **'This is where I will rest forever**. Here I will dwell, for it is my desire.'[1]"

He entered the city and prepared with joy for the big moment, and after several weeks he was called, per his words, to the yeshivah on high.

He was released in the year 5569 (1809).

≈ **He didn't want to give it to him ...** The love between human beings—here a teacher and student—is given primacy over immigration (*aliyah*) to Israel. Also, although HaYehudi haKadosh isn't ill, he dies when R. Peretz dies. It is understood from this recounting that there are relationships that are so inseparable in this world that when one person dies, the partner whose heart is broken may follow shortly.

1 It is a common thing for a dying person to discuss travel, as people may feel at some basic level that death is a journey and be readying themselves. They may talk of places they've been or even about something as seemingly mundane as watching cars pull in and out of an adjacent parking lot.

2 This was a pivotal moment in Torah, when the Gadites and Reubenites came to Moses and said they wanted to stay in Transjordan, where there was ample grazing land for their cattle, rather than crossing over into the Promised Land. Moses became furious, and the Gadites and Reubenites came back and volunteered to go into the Land as shock troops. It was only once Israel had conquered the lands that God had promised that they would return to the Moabite lands they were currently occupying. Moses agreed and the matter was settled.

In this story the Gadites and Reubenites wanting to stay in Transjordan to be near Moses's grave reflects the kind of devotional love that R. Peretz felt for HaYehudi haKadosh. The affectionate term "Rabbeinu" is used for both Moses and HaYehudi haKadosh, furthering this analogy.

≈ See Insight Spark: Cemeteries.

R. Peretz of Przysucha

The Przysucha school of Hasidism did not study Kabbalah. Instead of trying to understand God, they focused on trying to understand the human being. In this way, Przysucha declared itself in opposition to the dominant Hasidic movement of the time. Little is recorded of R. Peretz's life (d. 1814), but when he died his beloved teacher R. Yaakov Yitzchak Rabinowicz (HaYehudi haKadosh) said, "Really, Reb Peretz should have become rebbe after me, but since they knew in heaven that if Reb Peretz became rebbe, he would turn the hearts of all to heaven [and, thus, away from the human condition], he was taken from this world before me." Instead, R. Simcha Bunim of Przysucha became the successor.

R. Peretz of Przysucha wanted to travel to the Land of Israel and came before his *rav*, HaYehudi haKodesh, to get permission from him. **He** [i.e., his *rav*] **didn't want to give it to him**.

After a while R. Peretz became ill, and his *rav* came to visit him and asked if he still thought about the traveling.[1] He [i.e., R. Peretz] said to him, "It is written, 'The Gadites and the Reubenites owned cattle in very great numbers' (Numbers 32:1). They contended that they had a claim on their rabbi, Moshe Rabbeinu, may peace be upon him, and since he would be buried in Transjordan they didn't want to part from him.[2] Similarly, I see that Rabbeinu [i.e., HaYehudi haKodesh] will soon depart from this world, and I want to be together with him."

And so it was that in a short time both of them departed, may his merit protect us.

He was released in the year 5574 (1814).

≈ **why are you crying?** ... In this story we see an intimate moment between a husband and wife, with a glimpse into R. Simcha Bunim's attempt to comfort his wife. There is a repeated theme in these stories of a rabbi aspiring to have death be a time of celebration and attainment and this sometimes coming into conflict with the very human emotions of grief and loss. For R. Nachman it is his disciple R. Nathan and his students who cry out, feeling that they will be forsaken completely, and R. Nachman reassures them that he will remain with them. Here it is R. Simcha's spouse, and he frames his life and by implication their life together as a preparation for this very moment. There are many ways that people seek and sometimes find peace—often alongside real sadness and fear—with this time of transition and separation in relation to their loved ones.

≈ **so that I could teach myself to die** ... Perhaps what he's saying is that study of Torah deepens our understanding of life and prepares us either to embrace a faith in the next world or to accept the limits of our individuality and life, as Moses had to when he was not permitted to enter Israel. R. Simcha is now *ready* to die, a time viewed by Hasidim as one of ultimate unification with the Holy One, and thus a time for celebration rather than tears and sadness.

1 How can we further understand this idea that the time of death is joyous? In Joan Halifax's *Being with Dying*, she tells a story of joy and healing associated with death: "Years ago I spent time with an old Tibetan lama who seemed to be rejoicing as his death approached. I asked him whether he was happy because he was old and ready to die. He replied that he felt like a child who was returning to his mother. All his life had been a preparation for death. He told me that his long preparation for death had actually given him his life. Now that he was about to die, he would finally open his mind to its true nature" (Halifax, 9).

≈ **Elul** ... He dies in the Hebrew month of Elul, a month set aside for deep reflection on one's life and actions. Elul is also a month that evokes a vision of equality in love, due to a connection to the verse "I am my beloved's and my beloved is mine" (Song of Songs 2:16). We can thus understand his death in this month as fulfilling the ideal of attaining love of Torah, of God, and of a beloved partner, without one love undermining another.

≈ See Insight Sparks: The Timing of Death; Unification.

R. Simcha Bunim
of Przysucha

R. Simcha Bunim (Bonhart) of Przysucha (Poland) (1765–1827) was one of the main leaders of Hasidic Judaism in Poland. He became a Hasid of the Seer of Lublin with R. Yaakov Yitzchak Rabinowicz (HaYehudi haKadosh). After the death of Rabinowicz, most of the Hasidim followed R. Simcha Bunim as their rebbe. Among his followers were the Kotzker Rebbe (see "R. Menachem Mendel of Kotzk"), R. Yitzchak Meir Alter of Ger, and R. Mordecai Yosef Leiner of Izhbitz, among others.

When R. Simcha Bunim of Przysucha was approaching his time to pass on from the world, his wife stood over him crying. He said to her, "Silly, **why are you crying?** All the days of my life were only **so that I could teach myself to die**, and all of the Torah is that path to this. Now, as I approach this time, is it now the time to cry?"[1]

He was released on the twelfth of **Elul**, 5587 (September 4, 1827).

1 R. Levi Yitzchak of Berditchev (1740–1809) was one of the main disciples of the Maggid of Mezritch (see "R. DovBaer of Mezritch"). Famous for his compassion for every Jew, he was one of the most beloved leaders of Eastern European Jewry. He was known as the "defense attorney" for the Jewish people, because it was believed that he could intercede on their behalf before God. For this reason, it was expected that with his death he should be able to bring the Messiah, and therefore there must then be a reason that he did not succeed.

〰 **the holy ones ...** This refers either to great people who had died before him and would be there with him in the afterworld, or it may refer to God's angels. A parallel today might be that for some Holocaust survivors, the members of their families and good friends who perished at the hands of the Nazis are the "holy ones," who are waiting on the other side. Some survivors, as their own death approaches, have vivid visions and memories of them and may imagine meeting them again. They may also feel disappointment and guilt that even with the death, the sacrifice, of so many innocent people, the world is still a violent place and we have not yet achieved messianic peace.

2 He will not forget to pray for the coming of the Messiah and will thus bring about redemption.

〰 **Gehinnom ...** Here we have the first reference to *Gehinnom* that comes to communicate a possibility that the soul might go somewhere on its journey to the next world. See the section entitled "The Afterlife" in the introduction to this book.

3 Gehenna, also known as *Gehinnom*, is a term derived from a place outside ancient Jerusalem known in the Bible as the Valley of the Son of Hinnom, one of the two main valleys surrounding the Old City of Jerusalem. According to the Hebrew Bible, *Gehinnom* was where apostate Israelites and the followers of foreign gods sacrificed their children (2 Chronicles 28:3, 33:6). *Gehinnom* later became a figurative name in Hasidism for the spiritual realm in which people's souls are cleansed from the blemishes incurred by their conduct while on earth. According to most sources, the period of purification or punishment is limited to twelve months, after which the soul will ascend to the world-to-come, be destroyed, or continue to exist in a state of remorse.

R. Avraham Yehoshua Heschel, the Apter

Avraham Yehoshua Heschel of Apt (1748–1825), popularly known as the Apter Rebbe or Apter Rav, was born in Żmigród, Poland, and died in Mezhbizh, Russian Empire (now Ukraine). He was the direct antecedent of the great twentieth-century philosopher R. Abraham Joshua Heschel (1907–1972), father of the contemporary scholar Susannah Heschel (b. 1956).

Before the departure of R. Avraham Yehoshua Heschel, the Elder of Apt—our master, our teacher, and our rabbi—he shouted bitterly about our exile and why the Messiah was delayed.

And he cried and said, "The Rav from Berditchev[1] said before his departure that when he got there he wouldn't rest, he wouldn't be quiet, and he wouldn't let any of **the holy ones** rest until the Messiah came, but after that they entertained him in the courtyards and the high spiritual rungs until he forgot about it. But I," concluded the Apter Rebbe, "I will not forget…."[2]

Afterward he said, "*Ribbono shel Olam*, I know that my merit is not such that You would let me enter the Garden of Eden among the righteous. You might want to put me in **Gehinnom**[3] among the

(continued on page 107)

4 R. Heschel is posturing before God in saying that he may not merit the Garden of Eden, another name for the world-to-come, but that he cannot stand the thought that in *Gehinnom* he will be with those who block the coming of the Messiah, and thus he asks God to rid *Gehinnom* of those who went against God's will so that he can die and be in a place he can bear to inhabit. In truth, he is asking God to let everyone out of *Gehinnom* so that no one suffers except for himself. It is his final act of love.

∾ See Insight Sparks: Depression and Sadness; Talking with God.

wicked; however, You, *Ribbono shel Olam,* You know that I hated those who went against Your will, so how can I be there among them? Therefore I ask that You send out all the wicked of Israel from *Gehinnom* so that You can put me there."[4]

He was released on the fifth of Nisan, 5585 (March 24, 1825).

Depression and Sadness

On Simchat Torah of that year at the time of the *hakafot* there was the awesome story of the "fall" known to Hasidim, but concerning it they shared only veiled hints, softly spoken words with tremulous quaking.

—From the deathbed story of the Seer of Lublin

We do not know whether on that memorable Simchat Torah the Seer of Lublin was drunk and fell from his window, whether he attempted suicide, or whether he simply slipped and fell. Whatever the case, he is described as being in a bleak mood afterward and taking to his bed. This is in full contrast with the Hasidic idea that the day of death is a day of celebration. The rest of these stories mostly depict joy toward the end of life, accompanied by study, prayer, and even dancing and singing. Even R. Menachem Mendel of Riminov, who was in the Seer's group of those seeking the Messiah in the period following the Napoleonic wars, was doing *hakafot*, circling and chanting petitions nightly in the weeks leading up to the Passover before his death. The Seer's fall and dark mood are honored by his disciples as they remain loyally by him, while others undermined and mocked him, attributing his fall to a disappointment in his lack of success in bringing the Messiah.

There can be great disappointment for many people at the end of life. Sometimes it is because they really haven't had good fortune along the way or have squandered opportunities. Sadness seems like a rational response for this person, as well as for the person who seems to have had everything and is now suffering the sadness of loss and bereavement after a full life.

Thus feeling and expressing sadness in the face of loss of dignity, of control, or the impending loss of life is natural and important. We see this with R. Tzvi Hirsch of Zhiditchov, who is saddened by the realization that his study of the *Zohar* will end, and R. Yitzchak Isaac of

Zhiditchov, who dances and then also weeps. But Tzvi Hirsch continues to teach and seems to ameliorate his sadness this way. Yitzchak Isaac reads from the Torah and offers blessings to his Hasidim. These different ways of coping become integrated into life, especially with the supportive presence of family and friends.

Depression, on the other hand, as depicted in the story of the Seer, is a part of his soul, an identity that cannot go away or even lessen and likely added to the tenor and gravitas of his prophetic abilities. It can be important to recognize and to treat depression at every stage of life, and with an elder or terminally ill person it is still important to diagnose and to consider treatment so that people retain the potential to reflect on their lives and can say their good-byes. Some people will choose not to treat clinical depression, possibly because of the terminal nature of life at this point, in which case we can simply be present and honor that choice and, like the many friends of the Seer, continue to accompany him or her with love and loyal presence.

~ This is the only story in this collection that is fundamentally political in nature, despite the rabbi's prayer and dramatic death at its end. R. Rafael's life is about honesty and living and dying ethically in this world. He is not filled with visions of the afterlife; instead, he states his preference for death over having to lie and say he knew nothing of the death of the traitor and take his name off the document or be charged and tried himself for murder. Indeed, he and R. Pinchas of Koretz are well known in the Hasidic literature for the absolute commitment to the truth. R. Rafael's death is an insight into the centrality of ethics in his life, and God's alignment with this moral path is made clear in granting his death wish.

1 A Jew who was a traitor to his own people; probably an informer to the government, as this was not uncommon at the time.

2 The killing or murder of informers was not unknown at the time or in Jewish history (see "R. Israel of Ruzhin"). The burial in secret evokes the biblical story of Moses's clandestine slaying and burying of the Egyptian taskmaster and through this connection implies that the murder possibly was justified or viewed as a righteous act (Exodus 2:11–15).

3 An *agunah* is an Orthodox Jewish woman whose husband refuses to grant her a document of divorce or disappears without evidence of death; in the latter case, she is required to wait for his return and cannot remarry. As the death of the traitor could not be confirmed, the status of his wife was now that of an *agunah*—literally a "chained" woman—and without testimony from two witnesses, she would not be permitted to remarry. The petition would need to attest to the fact that her husband was confirmed dead. The catch is that in order to have known this, the signatory rabbis would have needed to know who committed the murder and where the body was hidden. The rabbis who signed this petition most probably thought they were performing an act of loving-kindness to help the traitor's widow, but in fact they were putting their own lives at risk with the Ukrainian authorities.

R. Rafael of Bershad

R. Rafael (ca. 1751–1827) was born in either Germany or the Netherlands and came to Bershad in western Ukraine as a young man. According to Martin Buber, one cannot consider Rafael separate from his teacher, R. Pinchas of Koretz: "In the whole history of Hasidism, rich in fruitful relationships between master and disciple, there is no other instance of so pure a harmony, of so adequate a continuation of the work. In reading the records, we sometimes hardly know what to ascribe to Pinchas and what to Rafael" (Buber, 20).

How did R. Rafael of Bershad depart?

Near Bershad lived a traitor[1] who caused great troubles for the Jews, until someone rose up against him and killed him in his wrath and buried him in secret.[2] In her wish for revenge, the wife of the murdered man made for herself a petition of release for an *agunah*.[3] And R. Rafael of Bershad and R. Moshe Tzvi of Severn gave her this petition, written and signed in their names.

(continued on page 113)

〰 **The woman …** Women are predominantly in the background in Hasidic stories, and here our female protagonist has the prominent role of villain, going to the non-Jewish authorities to try and seek vengeance on those Jews who killed her husband. That said, she is not alone, as we have a series of potentially "bad people" here: a traitor who is making trouble for the Jews, the murderers of the traitor, and finally the rabbis who are complicit with the killing, as they had to have witnessed some direct aspect of the murder or burial. Women are most likely to play a role in Hasidic literature when their legal status impacts the lives of the surrounding men. This story is a bit different because she manipulates the Ukrainian legal process to get revenge on the Jews who killed her husband. Sadly, it results in the rabbi's death. However, the rabbis do not judge her too harshly, at least in the context of this story.

4 By signing the document, the rabbis were appearing as guilty of or complicit with the disappearance of the traitor.

5 The government gave the signatory rabbis the opportunity to take their names off the petition so that they would not be charged with murder.

6 That is, he testified that the signature wasn't his.

〰 **Death would be better for me than such a life …** There are people who would rather die than live with dissonance, or in this case live with a court accusation of murder or being an accomplice to murder. R. Rafael had lived a life premised on truth, so had he lied to save his life, he would have been compromising his core identity. It is clear in the story that he would rather die than live with having to agree to a falsehood. This text helps us understand how a person near the end of life might pray to have life be concluded rather than live out a lie or a reality that goes against his or her convictions.

〰 See Insight Sparks: Clinging to God; Talking with God.

The woman went and delivered this petition to the government and thus posed a danger to the Jewish groups in this area,[4] and only after great effort, a final ruling went out that if the two *tzaddikim* swore that the signatures were not theirs, they (i.e., the government) would cancel the trial.[5] The Rabbi [Moshe Tzvi] of Severn did what he did to save the Jewish folk,[6] but R. Rafael [i.e., his cosigner], when he heard the final ruling [of the court], began to cry and shout, and in the end he announced that he had a recommendation.

He traveled to nearby Tarashcha; he contacted the *chevra kadisha*, threw himself on the floor, and said, "Master of the Universe, a lie has never gone out from my mouth. At the time of my old age should I now have sworn in vain—by no means! **Death would be better for me than such a life**. God of truth, take my soul!"

God heard his prayer and raised his soul to the high heavens.

He was released in 5576 (1816).

1 The conditions in heaven were supposed to be analogous to those on earth, and the rabbis often spoke of the "Heavenly Court" or the "Court on High." The earthly "court of seventy-one" refers to the Sanhedrin, a group of seventy-one rabbis who, in Temple times, heard cases and handed down rulings. After the destruction of the Temple, when Jews began spreading throughout the Diaspora, gathering seventy-one legal authorities became impractical; instead, consulting a simple court of three rabbis knowledgeable in Jewish law became the norm for settling legal disputes.

The "court of twenty-three" refers to the *beit din* of the priests. It was the court of Jewish law, comprising twenty-three senior priests, which oversaw the day-to-day operations of the Temple. In this way it supported the Sanhedrin in performing its duties. A common expression for "dying" in Hasidic life was to go to the Yeshivah or Court on High, and here, by referring to R. Uri's joining the Court on High, the story actually brings us inside this metaphor for the death of a *tzaddik* as a joyful and expansive event bridging a familiar experience in one world with a parallel experience in the next.

~ **Therefore, he will be elevated this very year ...** At times a terminally ill person will express a readiness to die and a desire to join those who have already departed. This can be very hard for the surviving family and friends, as it can seem like the person is *choosing* to leave or even desert family and friends. This story addresses this by describing similarly a rabbi who focused not on the living but on the dead to explain his own departure and justified his departure by describing a need for his presence in the next world.

2 Note that he died on the twenty-third and would now sit on the *Beit Din* of twenty-three.

~ See Insight Spark: Confession/*Vidui*.

114

The Angel of Strelisk

R. Uri of Strelisk (1757–1826) was famous for his style of prayer, which was full of fire, extraordinary fervor, and enthusiasm. Thus he was known as "the Burning [*haSaraf*] Angel." He was the foremost student of R. Shlomo of Karlin. Tens of thousands of Jews visited his minyan and joined him in prayer.

Two days before he departed, the Angel of Strelisk said:

"In the Court on High there is a Court of seventy-one and a Court of twenty-three,[1] and R. Michal of Zlotshov is one of the Court [of twenty-three]. However, because of his exalted saintliness he is not able to comprehend at all how a person would be capable of committing a transgression, God forbid, and because of this he is very strict. **Therefore, he will be elevated this very year** to become one of the Great Court [of seventy-one]. Thus a vacancy was created on the Court on High [of twenty-three], and because of this one of the *tzaddikim* of the present generation will have to depart from this world."

He was released on the twenty-third of Elul,[2] 5586 (1826).

Confession/*Vidui*

He instructed all the men of his community to come and then instructed his assistant to sing Psalm 139 for him, which concludes, "And see if a vexing way be within me, and guide me in ways everlasting."

—From the deathbed story of R. Shmuelke of Sasov

For the Hasidim, the returning of one's soul to God at the end of physical life is probably the most profound moment in a person's life. For this reason, for them and for many Jews, a special prayer called *Vidui* (i.e., Confession) is recited as death approaches. This prayer seeks God's mercy and asks for atonement. *Vidui* reminds the petitioner that what really matters is our relationship with God (see Insight Spark: Unification) and with our fellow human beings.

The term *Vidui* is familiar to many from the Yom Kippur liturgy, as the name for the communal recitation of transgressions. We learn from Torah, "When a man or woman commits any wrong toward another, thus breaking faith with Adonai, and that person realizes his or her guilt, then the person shall confess the wrong that he or she has done" (Numbers 5:6–7).

This same word, *Vidui*, is used for the prayer at the end of life, in which we ask God to heal us, to grant us forgiveness in death, and to offer protection to those who live on. It could be that a person has something particular on his or her heart or that there is just the need to ensure that everyone is feeling right with each other, leaving no words of apology or regret left unsaid. When the dying are not capable of reciting a prayer themselves, the custom is for someone else to recite the *Vidui* on their behalf. This is a good time to ensure that people speak about everything that needs to be expressed, even if it is unclear whether the dying person is still hearing.

In the same way, when we are in the position of saying the *Vidui* for someone who is no longer able to do it, we may be able to help someone else forgive and possibly find a greater share of peace with the dying person. Ira Byock is famous for his teaching on the four things needed to be said between people: "Please forgive me," "I forgive you," "Thank you," and "I love you," and with the end of life he adds "Good-bye." The *Vidui* is a precursor to this idea. It holds in it forgiveness and peace, gratitude, love and caring for family, and in its final words, an affirmation of God's role in the world.

The last words of the prayer are *Adonai, hu haElohim*, "My God is God." This is a reference to the first book of Kings, when Elijah wants to prove once and for all to the people that God, not Ba'al, is the one to whom they must be loyal. In a dramatic moment, God consumes the sacrifice that is offered by those loyal to Adonai and does not consume the one offered by those loyal to Ba'al. This story is retold annually on Yom Kippur as a reminder of Israel's eternal faith. Elijah's faith, however, was based not on experience, but rather on absolute trust. God frequently does not respond to our need to see evidence of God's will in the world; we are more likely to feel God's absence in the face of disaster and tragedy. By reciting this phrase in one's final hours, we call upon our collective memory as a people to remember experiencing God's immanent presence in the world and, in this moment when we are nearing death, to reassure ourselves of God's love and protection (Gillman, *Traces of God*, 8–9).

〰 **to thank you …** He is praying through psalms and using the psalm as his own voice. Reciting psalms is a traditional form of prayer that can bring comfort and hope in the face of illness and toward the end of life. Many psalms speak of life's most difficult challenges and conclude with a sense of hope and trust in God. The words of psalms can also provide comfort as a person moves between this world and the next. Psalms are recited by a *shomer* (guardian), who, according to tradition, keeps watch over a body between the time of death and the funeral service, and psalms are the poetry of the funeral service itself. Here we have a simple story where a person's life is guided by the words and spirit of the psalms—and in this way, he is held by tradition.

1   Psalm 119:62.

2   This statement evokes a line from Song of Songs 5:6, "My soul went out because of what he said."

〰   See Insight Spark: Talking with God.

R. Zusha of Plotzk

R. Zusha (d. 1840) was one of the leading figures among the *mitnagdim*, those rabbis who opposed the Hasidic movement. However, through his friend R. Shraga Feivel of Gritza, he learned about the Seer of Lublin and became one of his greatest disciples. Under the influence of the Seer of Lublin he became the rabbi and head of the court of the town of Schodlatz in Poland. The term "Avdak" is often used after his name is a Hebrew abbreviation for the term *av beit din kodesh*, or "head of the holy court."

R. Zusha, head of the holy court of Plotzk, lifted up his head at midnight and said, "I will arise at midnight **to thank you**."[1]

And with these words his soul went out with his word.[2]

He was released in 5600 (1840).

1   The difference between a rabbi and a rebbe in Hasidic life was that the rabbi answered specific questions of Jewish law and practice, and the rebbe was more focused on the spiritual life and souls of his people.

〜 **At least tell me the reason for this ...** The son is able to coax his father into speaking and communicating his wishes.

2   Unifications are a specific form of meditation in kabbalistic mysticism based on techniques developed by Isaac Luria (1534–1572). There were specific practices Luria gave to his followers based on their individual spiritual needs (Veale, 7).

〜 **it is better for me not to speak than to speak without unifications ...** R. Naftali seems content with silence here. From *Mishnah Avot* 1:17, "[Rabban Gamliel's] son, Shimon, would say: All my life I have been raised among the Sages, and I have found nothing better for the body than silence. And the essential thing is not the study [of Torah], but the doing [of Torah]. And one who multiplies words brings on sin." There are times when a person may simply want silence and accompaniment at the end, as words become too difficult.

〜 See Insight Spark: Unification.

R. Naftali of Ropshitz

R. Naftali (Tzvi Horowitz) of Ropshitz (1760–1827) was born on the day that the Ba'al Shem Tov died; because of this, the Hasidim of Ropshitz used to say that it was from the holy sparks that emanated from the soul of the Ba'al Shem Tov that R. Naftali rose to prominence. He became attracted to the Hasidic movement and traveled to the court of R. Elimelech of Lizhensk, becoming the first Ropshitzer Rebbe. He succeeded his father as the rabbi of Linsk and was the rabbi of Strizhov as well.[1]

Before the departure of R. Naftali of Ropshitz, he suddenly stopped speaking. And this caused great anguish to the members of his household and with those close to him, because they didn't know what had happened to him. And when he needed something specific, they weren't able to serve him, for they didn't know what he wanted—because he said nothing.

So his son, R. Avraham Chaim, came to him, and said to him, "My dear father, the way I see it you can speak, it's just that you don't want to. **At least tell me the reason for this**."

He opened his holy mouth and responded, "My son, from the day that I achieved understanding, I said nothing small or great without unification,[2] and now that my mind is weakened, I said **it is better for me not to speak than to speak without unifications**."

He was released on the eleventh of Iyar, 5587 (May 8, 1827).

[1] In the preceding story, one of R. Naftali's sons accompanies him up until the end. This story is about the death of R. Naftali's second son, R. Eliezer, thirty-three years later.

[2] A *baraita* is a Rabbinic teaching that was written during the Mishnaic period (ca. 10–200 CE) but was not included in the six-volume Mishnah. Nonetheless, the Rabbis of the Talmudic period (ca. 200–600 CE) often used a *baraita* as a proof-text for a later teaching. The *baraita* referred to here is a well-known one entitled "The Interpretive Principles of R. Yishmael." It refers to a classic hermeneutic principle called *davar shehayah bichlal*, "a matter that was included in a generalization." The Torah may state a law in general terms and then go on to give specific examples or instances; the examples are there to teach not just about themselves, but about the entire generalization. For example, Torah states that it is forbidden to work on Shabbat (the generalization). It also states that it is forbidden to kindle fire on Shabbat (the specific). From here the Talmud deduces that each category of work is prohibited independently on Shabbat. This application of the principle helps describe in a new manner the ways in which good might come to many people from a rabbi's death.

〰 **May his memory protect us ...** In this story R. Eliezer is expressing deep humility, saying that this isn't about him. When a strong central figure in a family dies—particularly one of great importance in a family—there can be fear that the moment of death is one where the meaning leaves a family, that there's nothing left to guide them. Here he is providing comfort in his final teaching by letting those with him know that while they may think that he has been the locus of the family, there's really been no difference between them in this world. Further, once he has actually died, his memory and teachings will still be there and will strengthen them.

[3] The original text of *Sefer haHistalkut* defines the year of R. Eliezer's death at 5633 (1872); later cemetery research has determined the year of death as 5621 (1860).

〰 See Insight Spark: Liminality.

R. Eliezer of Dzhikov

R. Eliezer of Dzhikov (d. 1860) was the son of R. Naftali of Ropshitz. Little is known about his life.

R. Eliezer of Dzhikov, son of R. Naftali of Ropshitz,[1] on the Rosh Hashanah before his departure said, "It says in the *Baraita* of R. Yishmael,[2] 'When a case that is part of a general category is singled out to teach something specific, it is done *not* to teach that just about itself, but about the entire category.'

"So it is with *tzaddikim*. While they are in this world they are included in the general category of 'world-that-is.' But when they leave that category, that is, when they leave this world, each life speaks well, not only for itself, but for the entire category—that is, for all of Israel."

May his memory protect us.

He was released on the third of Cheshvan, 5621 (November 4, 1860).[3]

∾ **The soul is Yours ...** At the very beginning of the traditional morning Jewish liturgy we thank God for God's faithfulness in returning our souls to our bodies, we then acknowledge God as the creator and shaper of our physical bodies, and finally we recognize that our souls have been breathed into us by God and always belong to God. At the end of R. Meir's life, he is relaxed, smoking his pipe, which is an indicator of physical relaxation and comfort, and he acknowledges God's role in the existence of his body and of his soul. He begs God for mercy and dies. This beautifully simple story emphasizes perhaps how a body and soul can be unified and integrated in life and that with death the goal is to find a new form of peace when the body ceases to exist and the soul is described as returning to God.

At the end of the life of a loved one, many families struggle with this connection between the body and the soul. If the soul is eternal and the body is ephemeral, how are they connected? If the body dies, does the soul die as well? If the body dies, but the soul lives on, how have they formed one cohesive entity created in the divine image?

R. Meir helps us understand that these morning prayers and those of the High Holy Days can help us live with the dynamic tension of body and consciousness being differentiated but intertwined in life. The prayers speak to our human experience of possibly feeling dissonance between our physical experience and the thoughts and emotions of our minds. People can feel young and yet see that their body has aged, or feel healthy and be diagnosed with illness. The prayers thus respond to the challenge of human experience and can support us in finding a balance between these two elements of our existence.

[1] This piece of the liturgy from the *Selichot* prayers, penitential poems and prayers recited or sung during the High Holy Day season, gives words to Rabbi Meir at this final moment and helps him express his sense of belonging to God and his desire that he be granted a merciful death.

∾ See Insight Spark: Talking with God.

R. Meir,
Son of R. Eliezer of Dzhikov

R. Meir Horowitz of Dzhikov (d. 1876) was the son of R. Eliezer of Dzhikov. He was the rabbi of Dzhikov concurrently with his father's being rebbe there; he then succeeded his father as rebbe. He died in Karlsbad, a well-known spa in central Europe. His teachings were published as *Imre Noam*.

R. Meir, son of R. Eliezer of Dzhikov, departed while he was sitting in his chair with the stem of his pipe in his mouth. He said, "**The soul is Yours** and the body is Your handiwork; have mercy on the fruit of Your labors."[1] And when he finished these words his pure soul went out.

He was released on the eighth of Tammuz, 5636 (June 30, 1876).

1 These deathbed words are attributed to R. Yochanan ben Zakkai (d. ca. 90 CE), an important sage of the Second Temple period and contributor to the Mishnah. The word "anything" implies "any worldly benefits," and the story continues, "even to my little finger" (see Talmud, *Ketubot* 104a). We can understand this as an expression of humility and love of God. It reflects an ascetic belief that was practiced by some Hasidim that elevated study and prayer over more physical engagement in the world. R. Naftali Chaim is stating that he never sought any earthly rewards (see also "R. Israel of Ruzhin") for his piety.

∾ See Insight Spark: Talking with God.

R. Naftali Chaim,
Son of R. Meirel of Dzhikov

R. Naftali Chaim Horowitz of Dzhikov (d. 1904) was the son of R. Meir of Dzhikov. He settled in Safed and eventually in Jerusalem. After his father's death in 1876, he refused to return to Poland to lead his father's followers.

R. Naftali Chaim, son of R. Meirel of Dzhikov, said before his death, "'Master of the Universe, it is revealed and known before You that I did not enjoy anything from this world.'[1]" And with these words his pure soul went out.

He was released in 5664 (1904).

1   This story, in contrast to all the others, is about the death of a student, who was beloved to his rebbe, a young man dying before his time and before the passing of his elders. The focus here is not on the death but rather on the rejoicing of the holiday. The rebbe senses the moment of loss and is shaken but then directs the community to continue with their rejoicing. This presents a reality in opposition to our current world experience where the death of a young person often stops us in our tracks and leaves us stunned and frozen like the disciples in some of these stories, whereas the death of elders can be less disruptive even when their passing signifies a great loss and they will be much missed.

〜 **like a man who had been shocked ...** This is an experience not uncommon to people at the time of death of a loved one; something sudden comes over us as our loved one is torn from the fabric of our lives, and it can be shocking no matter how prepared we are. And yet, on some level we must go on and manage the grief and loss and make life continue on even after it feels broken.

〜 **The war must continue ...** The "war" that must continue here is a reference to the way the Hasidim described the internal conflicts of each person. This war is the personal fight of an individual against the *yetzer hara*, the inclination of the individual for bad; this force is in constant battle with our instincts for good, the *yetzer hatov*. So here, as in war, when even though a leader falls, the battle continues, so too when fighting our negative sides, we cannot suddenly stop. The eternal engagement of a people seeking good must never stop; we must always carry on.

〜 See Insight Spark: The Timing of Death

R. Avraham of Olinov

Also referred to as R. Abi of Olinov, the rabbi in this story appears to have been a student of R. Naftali's but did not go on to become a rabbi with a following of his own. Thus, little but this story is known of him, not even his dates of birth and death.

They say that a rabbi from Olinov was one of the greatest lovers of R. Naftali of Ropshitz. He departed on Simchat Torah in Olinov.[1]

At that time the Hasidim in Ropshitz would go out dancing before the window of their rebbe as was their custom, and R. Naftali would stand by the window watching. Suddenly he raised his hand to signal that they stop, and he stood [still] for a few moments, **like a man who had been shocked**. Then he came out of it and said, "If you go to war and one of the leaders falls, do the soldiers flee like the faint of heart? No! **The war must continue**. Rejoice and dance!"

And he gave a sign and they began to dance as before.

Afterward it became known that this was precisely the same time that R. Avraham departed.

☐1☐ This story, the previous one, and the next all feature a rabbi very directly advising his students about how to understand and deal with death.

〰 **The *tzaddikim* that will come after us ...** At the end of life, R. Zev is trying to get his students to shift their longing for him to having a sense of what the future will bring. This evokes the dying person who knows her children are feeling her impending death, so she reassures them about the goodness of her life and the good that awaits them even after she is gone.

〰 **people long to see and gaze at his face ...** R. Zev is here trying to explain to his son-in-law and students how they will recognize a future *tzaddik*, which will be through the natural charisma the person will exude. In doing so, he links the greatness of the human spirit with God. This story may help us understand that in the face of the death of these special souls, the rebbes' followers had to have hope and know that the future would hold new leaders.

But he is also cautioning them that the great leaders will come later, not from the current generation. In the mid-1600s a great charismatic leader called Shabbetai Tzvi (1626–1676) arose in Turkey, claiming to be the Messiah. He was eventually proved to be a fraud, and the thousands who had become enthusiastic followers were crushed emotionally, a pain that remained in the souls of European Jews for many, many years. We hear echoes of that betrayal in this story, and 125 years after Shabbetai Tzvi's death, R. Zev is still providing assurance that there will be continued strong leadership.

〰 See Insight Spark: Ethical Wills and Advance Directives.

R. Zev of Zhitomir

As a young man, R. Zev of Zhitomir (also known as R. Zev Wolf; d. 1800) was drawn to Hasidism and traveled to the court of R. DovBaer of Mezritch, where he became a senior figure in the inner circle. From then on, he was totally devoted to R. DovBaer, who, seeing the skill and wisdom of his student, appointed him *maggid* of his hometown of Zhitomir. R. Zev's teachings were collected into the book *Or Hameir* ("The Shining Light"), one of the fundamental works of Hasidism and one of the earliest printed.

Before R. Zev of Zhitomir departed, his students and his son-in-law R. Shneur wept before him.[1] He said to them, "What do you have to cry about? **The *tzaddikim* that will come after us** will be much greater. And this is the sign for you: The one whom **people long to see and gaze at his face**, it is a sign that the Divine Presence rests upon him."

May his memory protect us.

He was released in 5560 (1800).

Ethical Wills and Advance Directives

And he sat up on his bed and instructed them to stand around him,
and he spoke words of Torah to them: about the pillar through
which one ascends from the Garden of Eden below to the Garden
of Eden above, and thus between each and every world how this
symbolism manifests in holy space, time, and people.

—From the deathbed story of the Ba'al Shem Tov

An *ethical will* is a document that describes a person's values—deeply held beliefs, ways of being that might hold hidden meaning, and accomplishments that are imbued with ethics. This is personal Torah, passing on what is most essential and helping express and possibly increase one's impact on this world. Ethical wills have a biblical origin, found in Genesis 49, when Jacob gathers his sons to offer them his blessing and to ask that they bury him in the cave at Machpelah in Canaan rather than in Egypt. And in Deuteronomy 32:45–47, "When Moses had finished speaking all these words to all Israel, he said to them, 'Set your hearts toward all the words with which I have warned you today. Charge them upon your children that they may observe faithfully all the words of this teaching. For this is not an empty thing for you—it is your very life, and through this thing you shall long endure on the land that you are about to cross the Jordan to possess it there.'"

The purpose of an ethical will today is to create a vehicle in which we can reflect on what we have learned in a lifetime—through both success and failure—that is worthy of being passed on to future generations. People might write such statements as the following: "I have learned that forgiveness frees not only the one being forgiven, but me as well"; "You come from a long line of creative souls who have had to struggle with their inner demons, but who have left great beauty—art, writing, music—as a result of the struggle. So my advice to you is to embrace the struggle and understand it as a gift"; or "It took me many years to understand the importance of the role my religious tradition might play in my life. I urge you to engage in that contemplation while you are young so that it is there to sustain you as you age."

An *advance directive* (also called a living will), on the other hand, is a document designed to help others know what healthcare decisions people would want if they were incapacitated and no longer physically or mentally able to make decisions them for themselves. More and more states have a universal form for advance directives and/or a POLST form (Physician Orders for Life-Sustaining Treatment) that travels with a person to guide any life-sustaining treatments.

Some of the key decisions covered in advance directive documents are as follows:

1. *Do not resuscitate (DNR) / do not attempt resuscitation (DNAR):* DNR/DNAR is a medical order to withhold cardiopulmonary resuscitation (CPR) or advanced cardiac life support (ACLS) in the event that a patient's heart stops or he or she stops breathing. For very old patients, CPR is rarely able to save a life, and brittle ribs can easily be broken, which can then pierce the lungs and lead to complications that cause further suffering. Some people will opt for mouth-to-mouth resuscitation but will specifically note "Do not attempt chest compressions." Without such an order, emergency medical technicians are legally required to perform chest compressions.

2. *Do not intubate (DNI):* A DNI order means that no breathing tube will be placed in the throat in the event of breathing difficulty or respiratory arrest. Under both DNR and DNI orders, a patient is provided comfort care. One can also choose to indicate "Use intubation and ventilation as marked, but short term only."

3. *Do not hospitalize (DNH):* A DNH indication means that the patient does not wish to be hospitalized for emergency lifesaving measures but will go to the hospital when needed for reparative procedures such as the setting of a broken arm.

4. Preferences regarding artificial nutrition, hydration, and dialysis.

Certainly none of the rabbis in *The Book of Departure* had such modern options as resuscitation, intubation, or hospitalization. However, they did on occasion turn the doctor away (see "R. Menachem Mendel of Kotzk"), predict and seemingly plan for the day on which they would die, and work to exert their will on their last days.

133

⟲ **the spirit ... began its bonding to God ...** This bonding, clinging, or cleaving to God at the very end of life is a statement made in a number of our stories and implies that the soul becomes one with God. The time of active dying was understood by the rabbis as a time when the soul actively begins leaving the body and reuniting with God, a time when the soul struggles with its new existence disconnected from a human form. Further, they understood this as a protracted period of struggle, perhaps taking as long as a full year.

⟲ **the *tzaddikim* who will be coming right before the Messiah will be greater than I ...** R. Aaron is trying hard to offer comfort to his family and followers, and maybe even himself as well, as he tries to let go of his responsibilities as the leader of a community. It can be very painful for someone who has guided and provided for a community to abdicate that role. Here we see him trying to offer a vision for how things will be even better in the future.

⟲ See Insight Spark: Unification; see also the appendix, "The Characteristics of Active Dying."

R. Aaron of Zhitomir

A disciple of Levi Yitzchak of Berditchev, R. Aaron of Zhitomir (ca. 1750–1822) wrote kabbalistic homilies on the Torah under the title *Toledot Aharon*. He taught "morality and pursuit of the service of God" through the intimate embrace of God.

As **the spirit** of R. Aaron of Zhitomir **began its bonding to God**, his students cried out a great cry. He said to them, "Why are you weeping? The ending of all people is to die."

They replied, "How do we not cry and not strike our heads? After you leave us we will be left like sheep without a shepherd, and the other righteous in our generation, their worship is very hidden and they will not reveal their practice as we are accustomed with you."

And he comforted them and said with these words, "You know that at the end of days **the *tzaddikim* who will be coming right before the Messiah will be greater than I**, and everything they do will be more special: unifications more awesome than what we did with our Torah and our prayers."

He was released in 5582 (1822).

1   There was a major epidemic of plague followed by cholera across the Middle East and Europe beginning in 1831. The original Hebrew in the text for "cholera," *choli-ra*, translates directly as "a bad sickness."

2   The cholera epidemic was killing tens of thousands in Asia and Europe, and people wrote to R. Tzvi Hirsch for help. They wrote to him because he was a great *tzaddik* and he helped many people, including, as we learn here, providing dowries for forty orphans. He gave life to people otherwise without hope.

~   **"Save us, our Rabbi!"** ... It is important even in the face of incapacitating illness to remember and see people as a whole and recall all the facets of who they are, and in this way to help them to feel whole at a time of brokenness. In this story, we see four levels of relationship, reminding us of the breadth and complexity of the dying person. He is *Rabbeinu*, "our Rabbi," being responsible to the community he serves; he is husband to a wife who has just died; he is father-in-law to one who may take over for him when he dies; and he is both student to Shimon bar Yochai and teacher to his own students, worrying over who will carry on his teaching.

3   R. Tzvi Hirsch reaches to touch his mezuzah, an object that can signify many things to people. It can make a home feel sacred, recall Jewish history, and also connect us to a larger community of people who follow this same practice for all of *their* diverse reasons. It can evoke a strong sense of God's protection going all the way back to its origins in the Torah, where the blood is smeared on the lintels (where now we place a mezuzah) as a signal to God not to kill the firstborn Israelites as part of the plague against the Egyptian slaveholders. Whether it's a mezuzah or our great-grandparents' rings kept in a jewelry box, an object can remind us of the past and family, a chain of people who offer wisdom and strength. At some future time we might pass them to our children to mark a new covenant in their lives. This is the power of the mezuzah—a covenant that never wears thin but is renewed as it is passed from generation to generation.

4   That is, "My death will atone for the sins of all Jews." When he says he is atonement for all of Israel, he is giving meaning to his death. In his life he helped and fostered life, and now he is praying that in death he will also foster life by stopping the epidemic, because if it is punishment for the people's sins, these will now be forgiven.

R. Tzvi Hirsch of Zhiditchov

Tzvi Hirsch (Eichenstein) (1763–1831) of Zhiditchov was a noted Talmudist and kabbalist and wrote insightful expositions on Torah. He was a disciple of R. Moshe Leib of Sasov, R. Menachem Mendel of Riminov, the Maggid of Koznitz, and the Seer of Lublin. He founded the Zhiditchov Hasidic dynasty.

In the year 5591 (1831) there was a plague of cholera in the world.[1] And letters to our R. Tzvi Hirsch of Zhiditchov arrived from across the Diaspora of Israel[2] saying, **"Save us, our Rabbi!"** Then one day when many letters had been given to him, as he stood in the *beit midrash* [study hall] wrapped in a tallit, he was greatly sorrowful, and as he was leaving, he reached for the mezuzah[3] and said, "I am the atonement for all of Israel."[4]

(continued on page 139)

5   The tallit that Rabbi Tzvi Hirsch is wrapped in provides another multifaceted layer of spiritual strength and protection. "Look at it [the *tzitzit*, or "fringes"] and you will be reminded of all the commandments of Adonai" (Numbers 15:39). With each thread and knot endowed with symbolism, according to Rashi, the four corners mean we remember our path every way we look. This protective canopy of God is understood a few lines later to be an augury of the rabbi's demise when one of the fringes is seen to be damaged.

〜   **R. Shimon bar Yochai** ... His wife has died, he is on his deathbed, and he reviews his life. He at once turns to his son-in-law, giving authority over to him as he tries to ascertain whether he has led a righteous life. After a pause of several hours, he turns, again, to a direct conversation with one who appears present to them but who, in fact, died earlier—indeed in this case, centuries before—R. Shimon bar Yochai. Whether it is a reaching into their deep psyche and emotional history or a premonition of the next world, as they near death people will at times feel the presence of those who have died before them or, even more commonly, speak of going to rejoin a deceased spouse or beloved relative. Perhaps this is one way we experience "being gathered to one's people," the phrase that is used in the Torah at the time of death, bridging worlds.

6   *Genesis Rabbah* 62:2 says, "When the righteous are about to depart, God shows them their reward." As Abahu saw the thirteen streams of balsam oil with which God was to reward him (a sign of comfort and prosperity), so Tzvi Hirsch is praying, still up until his moment of death, that he might bring salvation by ending the epidemic.

〜   See Insight Sparks: Liminality; Meditation.

On the Shabbat after this, when he was wrapped in a tallit,[5] he saw that one of the fringes was improper, and then he said, "There will be news."

And on the next Shabbat his wife departed [i.e., she died], and afterward he himself was ill and already he wasn't able to sit, and he lay down on his bed.

On the tenth day of Tammuz the disease struck him, and he asked his son-in-law if it were permissible for a person to find in himself a good quality. His son-in-law gave him a ruling that it was permissible according to Torah law. And he [i.e., R. Tzvi Hirsch] said, "I examined my life and searched all around and did not find good things in me, only that I married off forty orphans, and every time that I married off one of my offspring, I also married off an orphan-bride and provided a dowry for her and fed her at my table."

After some hours had passed he continued, "**R. Shimon bar Yochai** with your *Zohar*, who else will study you as I have? Nights and days ascend on high and mourn over me because who will treat you as I have?"

And afterward he taught Torah and explained the midrash "When he was dying R. Abahu was shown the thirteen streams of balsam."[6]

And in the midst of [his] *derash* [teaching] his soul went to heaven.

He was released on the eleventh of Tammuz, 5591 (June 22, 1831).

~ **Several years before his departure ...** Speaking far in advance about one's death can be helpful to those closest to that person. R. Yitzchak Isaac is described as standing on the threshold of the World of Truth. This evocative language challenges us to embrace honesty when having such conversations with others and to honor those whose vision incorporates death, as it might help those closest gain the understanding to respond with loving acceptance.

1 Proverbs 31:25. *Eishet Chayil*, "A Woman of Valor," is from the book of Proverbs and was introduced by the kabbalists as a song for a husband to sing to his wife on Friday evenings at the beginning of the Sabbath to honor her and also to honor the Shechinah—a name for God that is understood to be the presence of God that dwells among people and is thought to be a feminine aspect of God.

~ **was not an empty phrase ...** He is aware both of the centrality of his life in the lives of his community and of his coming death, and he begins preparing them for that event. The story tells us "he returned to the beginning of the *parashah* and recited it a second time." Why? To emphasize the point that they too can come to the point where they can "rejoice at the days to come." They not only can lose their fear of his dying, but can also rejoice in it.

~ **his joy was great indeed ...** He embodies the joy of knowing that his soul will soon cleave to God for eternity.

2 Proverbs 23:17.

R. Yitzchak Isaac
of Zhiditchov

R. Yitzchak Isaac of Zhiditchov (1805–1873) was the nephew and close disciple of R. Tzvi Hirsch of Zhiditchov until the latter's death. He later studied under R. Shalom of Belz.

Several years before his departure R. Yitzchak Isaac of Zhiditchov had become accustomed to speaking of his impending departure. And he would threaten the Hasidim, "In a little while he, himself, will be in the World of Truth, and he has already been standing with both feet on the threshold of that world."

On the last Simchat Torah his joy was very great, and on the closing evening of the holiday, which brought them into Shabbat, he was reciting the verses of *Eishet Chayil* in a holy and sacred manner, as was his way. As he finished the verse "and she laughs at the day to come,"[1] he returned to the beginning of the *parashah* [Torah portion] and recited it a second time. Everyone stood in amazement because our rebbe had never said one word of prayer twice. All the more so an entire *parashah*, and they felt that the ending—"and she rejoices at the day to come"—**was not an empty phrase**.

Even though [he knows he's going to die] **his joy was great indeed**, and he went dancing with the Hasidim in the middle of the dinner. Also on the next Shabbat our rebbe danced in the middle of the meal. And the brightest of his students saw in this *simchah* the joy associated with *tzaddikim* as they end their time in the world. For it was not the custom of our rebbe to dance on Shabbat, and his worship was only "in reverence of God—the entire day."[2]

(continued on page 143)

~ **words that were like a last will ...** R. Yitzchak was very conscious that his life was nearing its end, and for some people with this awareness, they might, like R. Yitzchak, feel passionate about using this time of full control to communicate their directions to those close to them, to ensure that their postmortem wishes are known and understood by everyone. It is critical that people be ready to receive these instructions, because it can help everyone adjust to the reality of possible imminent death and then afterward be able to honor the deceased by carrying out their wishes.

~ **his grandson ...** This tender moment with a grandson evokes the special intimacy grandchildren can have with grandparents and how it can also be a grandchild who accompanies an elder in a way that allows for tenderness, compassion, and an affirmation of legacy.

~ **praying for all the people close to him ...** Until now he has served to bring people closer to God, and now he is expressing an almost parental concern over his not being there in the future, and he's worried that they will now have to manage without him.

3 That is, the day following each of the three holidays of Passover, Shavuot, and Sukkot. Here he is referring to the day after Shavuot.

4 Rabbi Yitzchak is showing his personal strength in choosing to don tefillin and say prayers even though he knows he has entered the final days before his death. In the times during which this story was told, it was customary for Jewish men, particularly those who spent their days in study, to wear their tefillin all day long, though they would be removed before entering an "unclean" place such as a bathroom. He is speaking in the first person plural, perhaps demonstrating his unity with his son, even in the face of his imminent departure.

5 Literally, "bruised their feet," usually by having walked a great distance.

During the days of winter **words that were like a last will** were spewing out of his mouth, and on the thirteenth day of Nisan he became ill and went to a bed from which he would never leave.

One night during his illness **his grandson** R. Berish of Vortzki slept overnight with him and went to his bed on his tiptoes to see if he was sleeping and found him weeping, and his hand was holding his holy beard. He asked him what he was crying about. He replied that he was crying and **praying for all the people close to him** before his departure, in order that they resolve what each and every one of them needed to resolve in this world so that they shouldn't go up to the world-to-come in shame.

For the holiday of Shavuot, many Hasidim gathered in Zhiditchov. But that day [of celebration] was turned into mourning for them—their rabbi's illness grew stronger. However, a small number of Hasidim prayed with him at his home, where he went up to the Torah and read the Ten Commandments by himself; but his strength weakened and his voice could not be heard. All of them were weeping because of hearing his weak voice, which had always broken through to the heavens when he read the Torah on Shavuot.

On *Isru Chag*[3] as he put on tefillin, he said to his son R. Eliyahu, "On this day we truly are already exempt from [putting on] tefillin and from the *Tefilah* prayer, as we are departing from this crude world."[4]

When it [i.e., his illness] became a little easier, he said to his sons that he was sorry about the hundreds of people close to him who had made the strenuous effort[5] to come to him from far and near.

(continued on page 145)

~ **so he could bless them ...** He is exhibiting extreme gratitude to those who have traveled to pay their final respects. It can be very beautiful for family and friends to be present when a dying person has the opportunity to offer blessings, express hopes for loved ones and appreciation, and give and receive gratitude at the end of life. This time of blessing evokes Jacob's blessing of his sons and grandsons prior to his death (Genesis 49).

6 | In 2 Kings 20 and Isaiah 38 the story is recorded of a serious illness that affects King Hezekiah, who is told by God that he will die and he should ready his affairs. "Hezekiah *turned his face to the wall* and prayed to Adonai" (2 Kings 20:2; Isaiah 38:2), and God gives him fifteen more years of life. Perhaps the import of this reference is to make sure the reader understands that Rabbi Yitzchak could have prayed and extended his life if he chose, but even with all the sadness, he is ready to die.

~ See Insight Sparks: Blessing the Children; Purity; The Timing of Death.

And he instructed them to let them pass one by one by his bed **so he could bless them**. Thus most of the Hasidim passed before him in tears, and he blessed them with a nod of his head. The next day, at the beginning of nighttime, after the *Ma'ariv* prayer, he turned his face to the wall[6] and fell asleep, and the sound of his snoring was heard throughout the room. Suddenly the sound of the breath of his nose stopped and they saw that he had returned his spirit to his Creator—and his soul left in purity.

He was released on the ninth of Sivan, 5633 (June 4, 1873).

Purity

And in the middle of the teaching he told R. Avraham Shinas to complete the teaching, and then he left life to the living and gave his soul in purity.

—From the deathbed story of R. Aaron of Staroselye

A number of the rabbis in these stories are described in the moment of death as giving their souls "in purity." How do we understand this concept of purity, and what might it have meant in the world of these rabbis?

The first lines of the Ba'al Shem Tov's departure story tell us that he "did not lie down in a bed"; rather, he sat and meditated in another room. This is a vision of aging and nearing death that elucidates a heightened sense of one form of spiritual purity: lying in a bed can be associated with bodily secretions associated with illness such as vomit and feces, and also with sexual or intimate contact, and the rabbis were trying to disassociate the Besht from these physical impurities.

Too often as a person approaches death, it becomes much harder to achieve dignity. This can, among many reasons, be due to physical weakness, incontinence, forgetfulness, dementia, or diminishing senses—all of which could lead to physical challenges as simple as difficulty with eating and food dribbling down one's face, and discomfiture due to mental confusion. The text here is attempting to elevate the rabbi's dignity by taking him out of the context of physicality and honoring him for his spiritual fortitude during a time of physical weakness and increasing frailty.

It is important, however, to remember that this subjugation of the physical world—the world of impurities, but also of human touch and contact—should not be employed to *undermine* those for whom physical connection and creature comforts are essential toward the end of life.

We offer as an example a loving man, whose last real communication with his wife of more than sixty years was a long and gentle kiss. Not every person can or should move fully into the world of the intellectual and metaphysical in preparation or death. For many people, physical needs and the comfort of intimacy may become *more* essential as intellectual capacity becomes more limited and they move toward their final moments with dear partners, friends, and family.

1   A series of discourses on the Torah and festivals as viewed from a kabbalistic perspective.

2   This relates to a saying of Rabbi Yochanan: "R. Yochanan said: If a legal ruling is stated in any person's name in this world, his lips speak in the grave; as it is written, 'causing the lips of those who are asleep to speak'" (Talmud, *Sanhedrin* 90b). Inside this Talmudic quote is reference to Song of Songs 7:10.

⟿   **"Let these lips move in the grave."** ... By using this metaphor of movement by the body after death, he is evoking a powerful sense of people's presence being kept alive through their teachings—teachings that live on after their death.

⟿   See Insight Sparks: Liminality and Talking with God.

R. Tzvi Elimelech of Dinov

R. Tzvi Elimelech (1783–1841) was a nephew of the great rebbe Elimelech of Lizhensk, who foretold that his nephew would grow up to be an outstanding Torah scholar, which he did. He studied under the Seer of Lublin, the Maggid of Koznitz, and Menachem Mendel of Riminov. The Seer of Lublin told him that he was a reincarnation of the great early Torah sages of the tribe of Issachar.

R. Tzvi Elimelech of Dinov, author of the book *B'nei Yissachar*,[1] on the Holy Sabbath before his departure spoke at length on the subject of the world-to-come and on the saying of the Sages that one's lips mumble [move] in the grave.[2] And he pointed toward his holy lips and said, **"Let these lips move in the grave."**

And in those days he fell ill and departed to his world.

He was released on the eighteenth of Tevet, 5601 (January 11, 1841).

~ **We do not leave a son after us ...** In this paragraph R. Yuda moves back and forth between the first person plural and singular. When he speaks of not leaving a legacy in the form of a son, the "we" he references is most probably he and his wife, "the *rebbetzin*" of the next paragraph. The second "we" he refers to in discussing his spiritual and intellectual legacy is most probably his *chevruta*, his study partner—also possibly a lifelong relationship. He enters a state of intense concentration and prayer and in death is described in a unique way, as his soul being bundled up with God.

1 *The Book of Wisdom* was written around 1210 by the Rokeach, R. Elazar, who was born in Mainz and became rabbi of Worms. It is a mystical treatise on various names of God and the names of angels and on what are known as the seventy-three "gates of the Torah," referring to seventy-three methods of interpretation of the Torah.

2 He no longer intellectually understands the work on which he based his life work, and yet he is filled with the spiritual meaning. Elders can have wisdom that is deeper and more meaningful than the cleverness of a mind, as it is the summation of years of life, experience, emotional deepening, and integrated learning.

~ **in a big loud voice that did not sound like he had ever sounded ...** He is fully consumed by the passion of his prayers as he recites the Ten Commandments and then the paragraphs of the *Shema*, and he then launches into the final meditations prescribed by the Ari, bidding his wife to leave and not interrupt his intense final work. He is intent on grasping for and achieving his personal unification with God. At times, we are not included in a loved one's final moments and, like Yuda's wife, might be sent from the room.

3 See the almost identical language in "R. Shneur Zalman of Liadi."

~ See Insight Sparks: Meditation; Unification.

R. Yuda Tzvi of Razleh

R. Yuda Tzvi of Razleh (d. 1848) was a grandson of R. Yitzchak Isaac of Zhiditchov. There is next to no biographical information available about him.

Before his departure R. Yuda Tzvi of Razleh asked that they bring his writings on Torah to him. He studied them and said, "**We do not leave a son after us**; instead, I have set my stakes in *The Book of Wisdom*.[1] If I didn't know the author I would think that an angel of God wrote it. Believe me, I am now exhausting myself greatly trying to understand what I meant when I wrote these words."[2]

Afterward he began to recite the Ten Commandments (Deuteronomy 5:6–17) and the chapters of the *Shema* (Deuteronomy 6:4–9, etc.) **in a big loud voice that did not sound like he had ever sounded**. And the *rebbetzin*, his wife, entered the room in tears; he responded and said to her, "I beg you, go, and don't confuse me, because now I'm busy with the unifications transmitted by the Ari of blessed memory, in order to create oneness in these last moments."

And he finished his unifications and tied his soul into a single bundle with God.[3]

He was released on the ninth of Cheshvan, 5609 (November 5, 1848).

~ **the shofar of the Messiah ...** He became aware of the fact that his death was approaching and it was time to return to God. The root of the word for "return" is the same as the root for *teshuvah*, the process of recalling one's sins, setting things right to the best of one's ability, and asking for forgiveness from people and God. It is, of course, always time to do *teshuvah*, but no time is more poignant and serious than when physical death is approaching. This idea undergirds the Rosh Hashanah liturgy and ritual. Rosh Hashanah is a gentle way to practice preparing for death and then experiencing a new beginning, as is believed will occur in the next world.

1 For more on the time of divine yearning, see the note in "R. Yechiel Michel of Zlotshov."

2 Rosh Hashanah is close to the time of the fall harvest, and fruit may well be lying on the ground as they walk, thus inciting this simple question. One is obliged to eat three meals on Shabbat (Maimonides, *Mishneh Torah, Hilchot Shabbat* 30:9), and he may also be wondering if they can eat the fallen fruit as fulfillment of this obligation of the third meal (for more on the third meal, see the note in "R. Yechiel Michel of Zlotshov"). The third meal is also a metaphor representing the last part of his life and the idea that he is done and that any further fulfillment of mitzvot might need to be done by his children.

~ **wanted his sons to fill his position ...** He is expressing concern over his legacy and the need for someone still to bring the Messiah to earth.

~ **"A decree has already been decreed."** ... Note how different his response is to his friend a few weeks before his departure than to his wife just two days before his death. He is trying to prepare his friend for his death, but to his wife he expresses great ambivalence. He wants to live, but in the world-to-come. He is demanding that his friend understand and prepare for his impending death, whereas to his wife he expresses existential angst: He doesn't want to die, but he would prefer to live in the next world. It is as if with his words he is trying to convince his heart of what he is supposed to believe. With his death actually approaching, he seems to be losing some of his surety and defends his simplicity and innocence to God in his final words.

R. Israel of Ruzhin

R. Israel Friedman of Ruzhin (1796–1850), the great-grandson of R. DovBaer of Mezritch, lived in Ukraine and Austria and conducted his court with splendor. R. Israel had to flee Russia because an informant was known by the czar's government to have been killed under R. Israel's oversight. He reestablished his court in Austria, attracting thousands of Hasidim.

R. Israel of Ruzhin, on the Rosh Hashanah before his departure, said that he heard **the shofar of the Messiah**, hinting that his end was drawing near and that he was being called to return. A few weeks before his departure, R. Moshe of Kobrin came to visit him. On Shabbat [afternoon], at the time of divine yearning,[1] the two of them went for a walk in R. Israel's garden.

R. Israel asked, "R. Moshe, is it not possible to fulfill the obligation of the third meal with the fruits of the tree?"[2]

R. Moshe understood what R. Israel's words were hinting at: that R. Israel was going to depart from this world and **wanted his sons to fill his position**.

R. Moshe shouted, "Rabbi! You are still needed in *this* world."

R. Israel answered him, **"A decree has already been decreed."**

Two days before his departure his wife came in. He said, "How can I say that I do not long to live when surely I do long to live? However, I certainly do not [long] for this world, because this world is not worthwhile."

(continued on page 155)

3 *Peyot* are the side curls worn by many Hasidic male Jews in fulfillment of the commandment "You shall not round off the side-growth on your head, or destroy the side-growth of your beard" (Leviticus 19:27).

4 See a similar statement in "Naftali Chaim, son of R. Meirel of Dzhikov." See also Talmud, *Berachot* 48a.

~ See Insight Sparks: Body and Soul; Talking with God; The Timing of Death.

As his soul came to rest he grabbed onto one of the hairs from the *peyot*[3] on his head and said, "Master of the Universe, it is revealed and known before You that I did not benefit even by a hair's breadth from this world."[4]

He was released on the third of Cheshvan, 5611 (October 9, 1850).

Meditation

> When he became sick before his "departure," the Ba'al Shem Tov did not lie down on a bed, rather he had become frail and his voice was stricken, and he was sitting by himself in his meditation room.
>
> —From the deathbed story of the Ba'al Shem Tov

The history of Jewish meditation goes back to ancient times. In Genesis 24:63, the Torah states, "And Isaac went out to meditate in the field at the turn of evening, and he lifted up his eyes, and he saw." "He saw," that is, as he meditated he gained insight from on high. Note that he does this at a liminal moment in time, "the turn of evening."

Meditation is referred to in the talmud as a practice before prayer, branched out further as kabbalistic practices evolved from the early through the late Middle Ages, and became an entrenched Hasidic practice seen from the earliest stories about the Ari and the Ba'al Shem Tov. For an example of a meditative practice, we learn from R. Chaim Vital, a disciple of the Ari, who said, "Meditate alone in a house, wrapped in a prayer shawl. Sit and shut your eyes, and transcend the physical as if your soul has left your body and is ascending to heaven. After this divestment/ascension, recite one mishnah, any mishnah you wish, many times consecutively, as quickly as you can, with clear pronunciation, without skipping one word. Intend to bind your soul with the soul of the sage who taught this mishnah: 'Your soul will become a chariot ...'" (http://kabbalaonline.org/kabbalah/article_cdo/aid/380371/jewish/Meditation-on-a-Mishna.htm).

Perhaps the most prolific advocate and author of meditative practice was R. Nachman of Breslov in his *Likutei Moharan* and *Sichot Haran*. (*Likutei Moharan*, or *The Anthology of Rebbe Nachman['s Teachings]*, brings together the essence of Rebbe Nachman of Breslov's teachings—almost four hundred lessons relating to and dealing with all aspects of life.

Sichot Haran, literally *The Conversations of Rebbe Nachman*, is a compilation of insightful conversations, teachings, and insights heard from Rebbe Nachman during his lifetime, but compiled after his death by one of his students.) These books are a powerful endorsement of the power of meditation and its importance, not only to one's prayer and spiritual life but also to the work of caring for others. In addition, the Musar tradition—a Jewish ethical, educational, and cultural movement that developed to further ethical and spiritual discipline among nineteenth-century Eastern European Jews—has meditation techniques at its core. Today, as many Jews have begun to incorporate these older traditions into their prayer practice, meditation techniques have become quite ubiquitous, not only in the Musar tradition but also throughout much of the Jewish world.

There are many stories that document a meditation practice among the rebbes—from the Besht to R. Kalonymus Kalman Shapira (1889–1943), who authored a number of guided meditations (see *Conscious Community: A Guide to Inner Work*), to R. Menachem Mendel Schneerson. R. Shapira created a number of guided meditations for his students, including one that can accompany us as we face life's most painful realities. In the meditation, he asks the meditators to focus on their own deaths as a way of sensitizing themselves as they seek to comfort those who are mourning, grieving, or grappling with this final reality: "Consider what befalls each of us at the end of our days. In the final moments, a man looks out at his family and the world he must now leave. His body will go to ashes, to dust, to worms. And his soul? Does he know where his soul will go? He has never yet walked that path. His children surround him with the sound of their weeping.... He can hear everything, but he cannot respond" (Shapira, 28).

Meditate on this as you prepare to tend to the dying or to the seriously ill, as we are most present when we don't push away the reality before us but are reaching toward it. In the words of the poet Mary Oliver, "There are things you can't reach. But you can reach out to them, and all day long."

～ **dressed in new white clothes ...** This is a profound moment when R. David Moshe prepares for his own death. It is the holiday of Hoshanah Rabbah, the great moment of being saved, the word *hoshanah* appearing in the classic liturgical plea *hoshiah na*, "please save me," an emotion-laden entreatment to God. Hoshanah Rabbah is seen in the tradition as a second Yom Kippur, and a last chance to be saved from terrible fates. As is the custom in many congregations, the service leader puts on a *kittel*—the pure white garment in which a person is also buried. Here, R. David Moshe has new white clothes at the ready. He blesses his sons with the promise of a return to the Land of Israel, recites a praise to God, asks God to bless his soul, and he dies.

1 The understanding of angels in the *Zohar* and in Hasidism is that they are spiritual beings without bodily form. By donning white clothes and possibly reciting the words that angels are said to have used in praising God in the *Kedushah* prayer in the *Amidah*, the daily standing prayer, R. David Moshe is deemphasizing his corporal presence and is on his path to also becoming pure soul without a unique physical presence.

2 As Jacob blessed Joseph, "Behold, I die; but God will be with you and bring you back to the land of your ancestors" (Genesis 48:21).

3 *Nishmat Kol Chai* ("The breath of every living thing praises God ...") is an ancient prayer discussed in the Talmud (*Pesachim* 118a) and recited toward the beginning of the morning service on Shabbat and holidays. It speaks of God being close to us, in our breath, saving people from suffering, bringing the dead back to life, and healing the sick. These concepts are central to rabbinic thought. The words "Bless my soul, O God" said here form the beginning and ending words of Psalm 103 and are quoted toward the end of the *Nishmat Kol Chai*.

～ See Insight Sparks: Blessing the Children; Purity; The Timing of Death.

R. David Moshe of Tchortkov

R. David Moshe of Tchortkov (1827–1903) was the son of R. Israel of Ruzhin. His followers were one of the largest Hasidic sects in the region known as Galicia. He was an ascetic, preferring a life of study and prayer. Nevertheless, he was still a major figure in Central European Jewry, weighing in with Theodore Herzl on the future of Zionism.

On the night of Hoshanah Rabbah in the year 5664 [1903] at eight o'clock at night R. David Moshe of Tchortkov got **dressed in new white clothes** and sanctified himself like an angel of God.[1] Afterward he blessed his only son, R. Israel, and said to him, "You [will be blessed] to come with all the Jews to the Land of Israel."[2]

He began to say in holiness and purity *Nishmat Kol Chai*,[3] and his voice became weaker and weaker, and those standing close by heard only until the words "we will laud You and we will praise You." They guessed that when he reached the words "To David, Bless my soul, O God," his soul left in holiness.

He was released on Hoshanah Rabbah 5664 (1903).

1   Isaiah 38:14, "I piped like a swift or a swallow, I moaned like a dove. As my eyes, all worn, looked to heaven, 'My God, I am in distress; be my assurance!'"

2   At the time of his birth.

∽ **my soul would come down to this world ...** In the other stories that speak of "decrees," they imply that a decree has come down to indicate that it is time for the person to depart. Here, we have a discussion of a decree that a soul should come down and inhabit a new body. Indeed, this story attests to the belief that the soul exists prior to human life—that the soul is constant but the body dies. A midrash of a similar nature says that an angel strikes a newborn on the mouth and the newborn forgets all that he or she saw and knew as a soul (see Talmud, *Nidah* 30b), but clearly for R. Shalom this was not the case and his soul had memory prior to being placed in this body.

3   See "R. Naftali Chaim, Son of R. Meirel of Dzhikov," note 1.

∽ **anticipating the coming of my soul in this world ...** In the story of Rebbe Nachman he tells of the thousands of souls awaiting repair in the world-to-come with the death of the Ba'al Shem Tov, but here these souls wait in the physical world. How can we understand this? It might be referring to people whose lives he will positively affect with his life and teaching. He is anxious about his impending death, so rather than address his fear directly, he redirects to the time of his birth, finally recalling that God had told him he would leave this world "in peace." And then his soul rests, and he dies the promised peaceful death. It can be helpful to people to recall deeply held beliefs and times of peace and security in their lives.

4   From Genesis 4:12, God's curse of Cain to become a "ceaseless wanderer on the earth."

∽ See Insight Sparks: Body and Soul; Talking with God.

R. Shalom of Belz

R. Shalom (Rokeach) of Belz (1781–1855), also known as the Sar Shalom, "the Angel of Peace," was the first Belzer Rebbe, a title he held for thirty-eight years. He is known to have defended the Jews of his area before the governor of the district. When the governor asked, "Do you know that I am the second Haman?" the rebbe famously answered, "Luck wasn't on the side of the first one, either." The governor was so impressed with the answer that he promised to end the Jewish persecution. R. Shalom was succeeded by the youngest of his five sons, Yehoshua.

A half hour before his departure R. Shalom of Belz recited the verse "My God, I am in distress; be my assurance!"[1]

Afterward he said, "When I was told that there was a decree[2] that **my soul would come down to this world**, I said, 'I don't want it,' because I was afraid that I would fail, God forbid, in this world. Then the heavens showed me the reward for my mitzvot that I would store up in this world. Even so, I said, 'I don't want it; neither they nor their reward.'[3]

"I was shown several thousand souls that were coming stripped and waiting, **anticipating the coming of my soul in this world** so that it would repair them. Even so, I said, 'I do not want it,' because I feared lest my soul cause more damage than repair, until *Hashem*, may God be blessed, as it were, God, Godself in His glory, vouchsafed that I would enter this world in peace and that I would leave it in peace."

And, he concluded, "God, I am in distress, meaning, the souls that are in distress over their wandering the earth[4] without repair. As it were, be my assurance; You were for this—therefore, keep Your promise!"

And with these words his soul rested and his soul rose on high.

He was released on the twenty-seventh of Elul, 5615 (September 10, 1855).

~ **he got stronger …** In several of these stories we see a rabbi become stronger and take charge of the situation surrounding the end of his life. We see another example of this at the end of this story when he tells the *kohanim* not to leave. People sometimes rally prior to death and may seem to almost return to an earlier time of better health. This can be misunderstood as a recovery and more lasting than it is, so it is important to take the opportunity for final conversations and good-byes.

~ **Psalm 139 …** This is a psalm about how intimately one is known by God from the womb until *after* the end of life, and the psalmist asks for guidance. There is an element of *Vidui* (i.e., final confession) here as he asks God to forgive anything troublesome, and he does so by inviting all in his community to then join him in his experience of God's awesome qualities that according to the song will last forever. In having his community sing with him, he seems to receive a sense of peace and affirmation. We also can sing with a person or together as a family or invite a Threshold Choir to sing at the bedside and create intimacy and companionship in the shared experience of song.

1 This *piyyut* (liturgical poem), "The Glory and the Faith," is sung by the Ashkenazim (Eastern European Jews) only on Yom Kippur in the daily morning service. It praises attributes of God, and the refrain with which Rabbi Shmuelke's Hasidim respond is "to the One of Eternal Life." It is also a tradition to sing it during the *hakafot* on Simchat Torah, with *Zuvemen? Zuvemen?* ("To Whom? To Whom?") between the verses, adding a question in order to emphasize the answer.

2 The people helping him were the ones responsible for the operational functioning of the synagogue, sometimes called the beadle, the *gabbai*, or the shammes.

3 Because they knew he was dying and *kohanim* (those thought to be descended from the priests of old) are not permitted to be in the presence of a dead body, as it renders them impure and thus unfit for service to God.

~ See Insight Sparks: Clinging to God; Liminality; Unification.

R. Shmuelke of Sasov

We know little about R. Shmuelke of Sasov (d. 1858), only that he was a son of R. Moshe Leib Erblich of Sasov (1745–1807), the founder of the Sasov Hasidic dynasty. Moshe Leib was a disciple of Rabbi DovBaer of Mezritch, the disciple of the Ba'al Shem Tov, the founder of Hasidism.

R. Shmuelke, son of R. Moshe Leib of Sasov—his departure was a wondrous joining with God—with unfathomable ecstasy. Some hours before his departure, **he got stronger** and sat up on his bed and instructed them to give him his Shabbat clothes. He put them on and went from his bed by himself like a healthy man and sat in his chair by the table. He instructed all the men of his community to come and then instructed his assistant to sing **Psalm 139** for him, which concludes, "And see if a vexing way be within me, and guide me in ways everlasting."

And afterward he began to sing by himself in a voice hewing flames of fire the liturgical poem *Ha-aderet v'ha-Emunah*.[1] And all the people responded to him verse after verse. And when he finished he fainted and they had to put him back in bed. And immediately he began to die, and the *shamashim*[2] told the *kohanim* to go out,[3] and suddenly he woke up and said, "They don't need to go, and when they need to, I will tell them."

And so it was. And he left and passed from the world of the living.

He was released in 5618 (1858).

Liminality

Afterward he put on a tallit and tefillin and prayed until he
reached the *Shema,* and at the verse "And you shall look at it,"
he started shouting these words many times.

—From the deathbed story of R. Yechiel Michal of Glina

We need comfort during unsettling times of change, and so we seek
reassurance. For this reason, we hang mezuzot on our doorposts and find
a reminder of security as we transition from the safety of our homes into
the outside unknown world, we offer prayers at dusk and at dawn as the
world changes around us, and we mark the cycles of the moon in community with prayers. There is a long list of how our tradition offers us a
handrail at these times of ascent and descent. But what do we do when
a person is caught in the circular door, when he or she has for all intents
and purposes left us but remains physically in this world? Perhaps we
have a choice. We can sit and mourn the person's absence and grieve
over the one who is no longer here with us, or with great strength we
can embrace the unknown, and the person caught between worlds, and
perhaps even find God's presence as we search the maze or at times the
shallow depths of altered realities.

Unification

> And he finished his unifications and tied his soul into a single
> bundle with God.
>
> —From the deathbed story of R. Yuda Tzvi of Razleh

When Hasidim speak of unification, they are speaking of an ideal state of being in which our individual reality is totally inseparable from the Divine—two become one, the parts become the whole. The Bible teaches, "There is none but Me. I am Adonai and there is none else, I form light and create darkness, I make weal and create woe—I Adonai do all these things" (Isaiah 45:6–7).

The idea is that the singularity of God's existence should become our sole reality. That is to say, the *only* reality is the reality of God. There is no nature, there is no me, there is no you—all of existence is the deepest expression of God. This was formulated by the Ari in a *kavanah* (a meditation of intent) for the purpose of focusing one's prayer: "For the sake of the Holy One, blessed be God and God's Shechinah" (in Rabbinic Aramaic, *L'shem yichud b'rich hu u'Shechinateh*). The idea is that our prayer should serve to unite God's presence on heaven and earth. The concept of unification is so fundamental to Hasidism that it can be thought of as an underpinning to every story in this book. It helps us understand that the experience of death for the *tzaddik* is one of serving to further this unification. The dying person is gathered to God, like a drop of rain falling into a lake.

1 This is a reference to Kalonymus Kalman Epstein (b. 1753), also known as the Mei'osh, whose collected sermons were published as *Ma'or va-Shemesh* (*Light and the Sun*).

∿ **Welcome, my teacher ...** He is welcoming his teachers, who have predeceased him, and is asking them to accompany him at this final time in his life. This story is a retelling of a Talmudic story (*Berachot* 28b) in which R. Yochanan ben Zakkai tells his students to "prepare a chair for Hezekiah, the king of Judea, who is coming from the upper world to accompany me." So, it can be meaningful to remember those who are or have been the most important people in our lives, through their teachings or influence, and to "invite them in" to support and provide strength to the dying person. They exist in our thoughts, in who we have become through their impact on us, and in our memories and perhaps even in a different dimension of time and space, which may become more accessible to people as they themselves near death.

2 "Kalmish" was the nickname of Kalonymus Kalman Epstein (see note 1).

∿ **And you shall look at it ...** This is his spiritual intention as he dies: the centrality of God's commandments in his life. He dies proclaiming the importance of remembering.

3 This is a reference to the third paragraph of the *Shema* (Numbers 15:37–41), where we find the command to put a blue thread in each of the tassels on the corners of one's garments as a reminder of God's commandments and the injunction to keep them to achieve holiness.

∿ See Insight Spark: Liminality.

R. Yechiel Michal of Glina

Yechiel Michal of Glina (1829–1908) was also called the Aruch haShulchan, after his major written work. He was a Lithuanian rebbe born into a family of wealthy contractors for the czarist Russian army in what is now Belarus. He first became rebbe of Novozybkov, a town largely populated by Lubavitch Hasidim, and later of Navahrudak, where he would serve until his death. He was a great advocate of charitable giving and was close to R. Shmuel Salant, chief rabbi of Jerusalem.

Before his departure, R. Yechiel Michal of Glina (nephew of R. Kalonymus,[1] author of *Ma'or va-Shemesh*) gathered his strength and sat up on his bed and said, "**Welcome, my teacher**, R. Ezekiel of Kahalov." And he instructed them to put a chair next to his bed.

Again he said, "Welcome, my teacher, R. Kalmish[2] of Krakow (the Mei'osh)," and instructed them to place another chair.

Afterward he put on a tallit and tefillin and prayed until he reached the *Shema*, and at the verse "**And you shall look at it**,"[3] he started shouting these words many times. And his soul departed in purity.

1 Menachem Mendel possibly suffered a severe depression after he shared what might have been a blasphemous teaching with his Hasidim on a Sabbath eve in 1839; this precipitating event caused him to retreat to his study for the last nineteen years of his life. He chose to die alone and without help.

~ **kicked out ...** There are times when patients no longer want company or activity and want time alone—for a variety of possible reasons. They may simply feel fully at peace alone or better able to focus their thoughts. There also are times when people who are actively dying will ask those close to them to leave so that they can not only be alone, but die alone. For some of these people it may be easier for them to have you leave than for them to experience leaving you.

~ **instructed them not to bring a doctor ...** Menachem Mendel of Kotzk is asserting himself at the time of death and taking control of the situation. Here, even though people bring in a doctor, he rejects care and refuses his medications. This is not an uncommon situation in our modern society. Some people toward the end of life for many diverse reasons will refuse all treatment, and others will opt solely for comfort care, and the palliative- or hospice-care staff will stop all curative treatments and retain only those that help with pain or agitation.

~ **he completely stopped talking ...** This seems in line with his character as someone who chose seclusion for twenty years. Like R. Naftali of Ropshitz, here is another rabbi who stops speaking when he is near death. *Mishnah Avot* 1:17 says, "[Rabban Gamliel's] son, Shimon, would say: 'All my life I have been raised among the Sages, and I have found nothing better for the body than silence. And the essential thing is not the study [of Torah], but the doing [of Torah]. And one who multiplies words brings on sin.'" There are times when we simply accompany the dying person in silence.

~ See Insight Sparks: Body and Soul; The End of Desire.

R. Menachem Mendel
of Kotzk

Better known as the Kotzker Rebbe (1787–1859), R. Menachem Mendel of Kotzk was a student of R. Simcha Bunim of Przysucha and upon R. Simcha's death attracted many of his followers. After 1839 he lived in seclusion for the last twenty years of his life.[1] He continues to be well known for his practical philosophies and witty sayings. The Kotzker Rebbe is viewed as the spiritual forebear of the Ger dynasty in Poland and the teachings of its founder, Rabbi Yitzchak Meir Alter, grew out of his teachings (see "R. Yitzchak Meir, Master of the *Chidushei haRim*").

R. Menachem Mendel, the aged rabbi from Kotzk, at the time that he became ill with the sickness that killed him, he **kicked out** all the people who had been with him and **instructed them not to bring a doctor**. They paid no attention to his words and brought a doctor. But he didn't respond to him and refused to take medicine.

Several days before his departure, **he completely stopped talking** and did not want to answer any questions, and they did not hear from his mouth even a simple statement. And so, his spirit ascended on high.

He was released on the twenty-third of Shevat, 5619 (January 28, 1859).

1 Literally, "The Innovative Teachings of the Rim" (an abbreviation for *R. Yitzchak Meir*).

2 For more on the time of divine yearning, see "R. Yechiel Michel of Zlotshov," note 5.

3 For more on the third meal, see the note in "R. Yechiel Michel of Zlotshov."

~ **He called to him ...** There's a sweetness to this in that as he is dying he focuses on the youngest, the one who will survive him. Torah becomes a means of connection in the moment and will live on in his grandson.

~ **He covered his face ...** He is taking charge and preparing himself physically for death, as at the moment of death it is customary to cover the deceased with a sheet (see "Jewish End-of-Life Practices" in the introduction to this book). Also, perhaps, he doesn't want his young grandson to see him die.

4 A *tallit katan* (literally, "a small prayer shawl") is a simple fringed garment worn on the torso, under the clothing of many pious Jews. It is worn in fulfillment of the commandment "Speak to the Israelites and instruct them to make for themselves fringes on the corners of their garments throughout the ages" (Numbers 15:38).

~ See Insight Sparks: Blessing the Children; Liminality.

R. Yitzchak Meir, Master of the *Chidushei haRim*

R. Yitzchak Meir (Rotenberg-Alter, 1789–1866) was the first rebbe of the Ger (Poland) Hasidic dynasty. A descendant of the great medieval commentator Rashi, R. Yitzchak came from a distinguished line of German and Polish rabbis and was himself known as a great Talmudic scholar. He was close to the rebbes of Koznitz and eventually to R. Simcha Bunim of Przysucha, whose close disciple he became. After the death of R. Simcha, he became a disciple of R. Menachem Mendel of Kotzk, whose sister he married.

The soul of R. Yitzchak Meir, master of the *Chidushei haRim*[1] left at twilight on Shabbat, the time of divine yearning.[2]

He sat on the chair and washed his hands for the third meal.[3] He sliced, blessed, and tasted. His face began to change, and all the people saw that the time of parting was approaching. They were all moved to weeping and much ado.

R. Yitzchak Meir felt that one of his grandsons, who was then a small boy, was standing idle. **He called to him** and said to him, "While everyone is busy with this confusion, you are idle with no Torah. Bring a Gemara and I will give you a lesson."

He covered his face with a *tallit katan*[4] and departed to eternal life.

He was released on the twenty-third of Adar, 5626 (March 10, 1866).

〰 **During the last years of his life ...** He seems to have been ready to leave this world for a particularly long time. The Job reference may imply that his life was not so happy and that he felt that he had completed his work on earth. At times a person will ask, "Why have I not died already?" And we need to hear that emotion and possibly even ensure that a person has a valid advance directive document that reflects this clear preference if it is indeed aligned with his or her values.

1 Job 30:23. Similarly, the preceding line in Job is, "For I know that You will bring me to death."

〰 **I fear lest they not take any more *tzaddikim* from this world ...** R. Shlomo fears that others will have departed and he will be left among the living. Some elders who outlive their parents, siblings, friends, and maybe even a few younger relatives can feel increasingly detached from life and as if they might even have been forgotten by God or by death. A person might yearn to join those who have passed on, partially out of a sense of having been left behind.

2 See "R. Yechiel Michel of Zlotshov," note 4, for an explanation of this line.

〰 **his spirit had already been returned to his God ...** Rabbi Shlomo was walking, praying, speaking, and studying up until the moment of this death. In today's medical environment, many people lose their emotional and intellectual presence before their physical death; their body will still have vital signs, but they appear no longer to be present. This is also true for those who have advanced dementia; we may have lost the original person long before the actual physical death, and it can be important to recognize when a person's consciousness is actually fading or becoming distorted, so that we can say some of our good-byes and give him or her opportunity for this as well.

R. Shlomo,
the *Kohen* of Radomsk

R. Shlomo haKohen (Rabinowicz) (1801–1866), the first rebbe of the Radomsk Hasidic dynasty, is considered one of the great Hasidic masters of nineteenth-century Poland. He is known as the Tiferet Shlomo, after the title of his major work, a classic in Hasidic literature. He married Gitele, a pious woman who fasted every Monday and Thursday (market days, on which the Torah is read in synagogues); she lived to the age of ninety-two. R. Shlomo had a beautiful singing voice and was renowned as a cantor and a composer of *niggunim* (wordless melodies). His music was said to infuse his prayers with great emotion and joy and roused his Hasidim to great fervor in their praying.

During the last years of his life they recognized that R. Shlomo, the *Kohen* of Radomsk, was preparing himself for [death,] "the appointed house for all who live."**1**

On the holy Sabbath of the twenty-third of Adar, R. Yitzchak Meir of Ger, master of the *Chidushei haRim*, departed, but the matter became known to R. Shlomo only on the following Thursday. He said to his son-in-law R. Lippman, "**I fear lest they not take any more *tzaddikim* from this world**." And he took his own beard in his hand and said, "You see that also *my* beard is white."

In the evening, when everyone went out of his room, he walked back and forth with great agitation, caught in his holy ideas. And when it was two [minutes] after midnight, "the angels overcame the mortals, and the holy ark was captured."**2**

When they entered his room, they saw that he was sitting in his chair but **his spirit had already been returned to his God**.

(continued on page 175)

3 Leviticus 16:1. Once he has figured out that God took both of Aaron's sons, he becomes comfortable that he and R. Yitzchak could both be taken by God as well.

〜 See Insight Sparks: Clinging to God; Ethical Wills and Advance Directives; Liminality.

His head was resting on a copy of the *Zohar* open to the *parashah* beginning, "After the death of the two sons of Aaron."[3]

He was released on the twenty-ninth of Adar, 5626 (March 16, 1866).

〰️ **this year he would depart from this world ...** We have a repeated theme in these stories of people knowing that they are going to die. Similarly, in life at times we meet people who have a sense that they are dying, and they might have made peace with it or they might be wrestling and possibly in strong denial. With very old people death is inescapable, and it can become an important part of our life's work to integrate this reality into our life wisdom and to then be able to help others through the loss and sadness of our own impending death. This can take the form of sharing wisdom, giving and receiving blessings, and possibly communicating a profound sense of connection that can carry beyond death.

[1] The father of his daughter-in-law.

[2] A *goses* is a person who is actively dying and who is expected to die within seventy-two hours.

[3] This is a firm point of Jewish law reinforced in the Mishnah, the Talmud, the *Shulchan Aruch*, and the *Mishneh Torah*: "The *goses* is like the living in every respect." While the purpose of this law is to honor the person's full rights and protect the person from having his or her rights compromised, one implication that is also drawn is that if a *goses* is like the living in every respect, then he or she must be obligated to all the mitzvot (e.g., recitation of the *Shema*), when in fact that is not the intention of the legal rulings and not realistic for most people just hours or days from death.

〰️ **How does a person merit a departure like this! ...** Many people have had an image of what they would want their deaths to be like. Here R. Avrahamli recalls the death of a rebbe who had a Talmudic discussion, recited the *Shema*, and died. He is wishing his death would be like this.

Talking with a person about the actual event of dying, the physiological process and how it might be experienced, and also the spiritual elements and planning can be profoundly healing in advance of death. This might involve playing particular music a person wants to be hearing, having certain people present, or reading poetry or prayers that are beloved by a person.

R. Avrahamli of Sochaczow

R. Avrahamli of Sochaczow (also Avrahameleh; 1839–1910) was the author of *Eglei Tal* and *Avnei Nezer* on the *Shulchan Aruch*, the great code of Jewish law. He was greatly influenced by his father-in-law, R. Menachem Mendel of Kotzk, and later by R. Yitzchak Meir. As a result of a string of political events he lost his state license to be a rabbi, and though he maintained the position of Hasidic rebbe, he lost his position as the official rabbi of Sochaczow.

A few weeks before his departure, the Gaon R. Avrahamli of Sochaczow, son-in-law of the Alter Rebbe of Kotzk, said to his son R. Shmuel that **this year he would depart from this world**.

At the same time he told his *mechutan*,[1] the Rav of Kishnez, that at the time that the Gaon R. Livush Charif was a *goses*[2] he was wondering if a *goses* was like a living person and obligated regarding recitation of the *Keriat Shema* or if a *goses* was like the dead and exempted from the recitation of *Keriat Shema*. And he ruled that a *goses* was like a living person,[3] and he recited the *Shema* and departed. And R. Avraham [i.e., R. Avrahamli] moaned, "**How does a person merit a departure like this!**"

The same day that his soul arose to heaven, he prayed and put on his tefillin and in the middle of the *Shemoneh Esrei* prayer when he reached the prayer [that ends with the blessing "Blessed are You, O Adonai,] who gathers the dispersed of His people Israel," he instructed them to remove his tefillin from him.

He began [the process of] dying. And his sons and students stood about him in tears. But he, his mind was clear, and he was silent and said nothing. One of his grandchildren saw that one of his legs was hanging outside of the bed, and he wanted to put it

(continued on page 179)

[4] This is the Aramaic of the quote from Job 30:23 that appears in the preceding story.

[5] *Zohar*, part I, *Vayechi*, 248b. A bed often appears to the kabbalists as a metaphor for the Shechinah, God's indwelling presence, as the word *Shechinah* could literally be understood as a resting place. The biblical citation quoted relates to the death of Jacob (Genesis 49:33).

∾ **the law of not moving a *goses* ...** He understands his grandson's movement to mean that he is coming to help him move his legs, but he also senses that he is about to die. According to the *Shulchan Aruch* (339), one does not move a dying person lest one hasten his or her dying, so R. Avrahamli signals his grandson *not* to come help lest he violate that law. He is both teaching *and* protecting his family until the end and having exactly the departure for which he had hoped.

[6] See note on "in a kiss" in "The Ari—Isaac ben Solomon Luria Ashkenazi" for an explanation of this line.

∾ See Insight Sparks: Blessing the Children; Body and Soul; Kindness; Liminality; The Timing of Death.

back on the bed: as the *Zohar* says, "And he gathered his leg to the bed—for he dwelled in the place for all who live;[4] when he was about to depart from the world, he rested his feet on the bed, was gathered in, and departed from the world, as it is written: *he expired and was gathered to his people.*"[5]

He [i.e., R. Avrahamli] understood his [grandson's] movement and signaled [to his grandson] that he should not touch him, according to **the law of not moving a *goses***. So he gathered his [own] legs and sent out his soul with a kiss.[6]

He was released on the eleventh of Adar.

Blessing the Children

"My sons, hold yourselves together as one, and thereby you will overcome everything."

—R. DovBaer of Mezritch

It is a Jewish custom for parents to bless their children every week on Friday evening near the onset of Shabbat, saying, "May God make you like Ephraim and Menasheh; may God make you like Sarah, Rebecca, Rachel, and Leah," followed by the Priestly Blessing. But what of a blessing from a deathbed? Certainly if we wish for God's blessing for our children as the Sabbath comes in each week, as we approach the end of life all the more so we might have blessings to express.

As quoted above, in the deathbed story of DovBaer of Mezritch, the rebbe gives a blessing for unity to his son and his disciples. It is his blessing to his children, both those born to him and those who have become sons through love and commitment. What does this blessing reflect? It seems that he understands that at times children can become fractured and at odds with one another after the death of a parent, and he is charging them with not letting this happen.

"And Jacob called to his sons and said, 'Gather together that I may tell you what shall befall you in the days to come'" (Genesis 49:1). Before Jacob died, he blessed each of his twelve sons and their families. In addition, as a special reward to Joseph, who had remained righteous throughout his life in Egypt, he gave a special blessing to Joseph's sons. Ephraim and Menasheh were the only ones to grow to maturity outside of the Land of Israel and the first biblical brothers to live in harmony with each other all their lives. These two stories together teach us what we might see as an essential element of the deathbed blessing: helping bring about peace and unity among those who will soon be bereaved, so that they can draw strength from one another after their loved one has died.

Kindness

"Now it is time for you to reciprocate."
—The Ba'al Shem Tov

We are taught that the kindness we show toward a dead person by caring for the body, burial, and eulogizing is of the highest sort because it will clearly never be reciprocated by the deceased. This would be true also of a dying person. The Ba'al Shem Tov turns this on its head by demanding that the kindness he has done up to this point be returned to him, thus making it a repayment of a debt rather than a freewill offering. We often feel the desire to give fully to people when they are vulnerable. Why did the Besht have to say this to his followers? Shouldn't they have known already, or is it perhaps naming and articulating an extremely challenging shift in their relationships? Regarding those who have been strongest in our lives, we may be blind to this new helplessness and not see how much they suddenly need us. Until now his followers have looked to the Besht for care, guidance, and wisdom. In this moment he is telling them that this will no longer be so and that he will now be dependent on them. By framing it in the language of *chesed* and making it crystal clear, he is helping his students who may be denying this transition because they are so fond of his leadership. This is a poignant and tender moment for many people, and one that often happens slowly over time without the opportunity to name it or mark the transition.

1 See "R. Menachem Mendel of Riminov." R. Menachem Mendel seemed to have lost hope at the end of life, but here is remembered for his messianic hope and commitment to bringing on the time of the Messiah.

2 This is an interesting string of stories that show how a succession of rebbes were unable to resist the diversions that were put before them in the world-to-come, to which each succumbed and which prevented them from bringing on the time of the Messiah. Beginning at this point, the action all takes place in the world-to-come, so we must speculate on how information about the world-to-come was received. Perhaps the stories were revealed to R. Yekutiel in a dream, which by the end of this story seems to have made him all the more determined to achieve his goal of bringing the Messiah.

3 In Hungary.

R. Yekutiel Yehudah, Master of the *Yitav Lev*

R. Yekutiel Yehudah (Teitelbaum) (1808–1883) was a Hasidic rebbe in Austria-Hungary. He was known as the Yitav Lev, an eponym after his Torah commentary, which he originally published anonymously.

R. Yekutiel Yehudah, author of the *Yitav Lev*, told a story that he heard from the mouth of R. Chaim of Tzinz, that *he* told, that the Rav (the Moharan of Ropshitz) told, that the rabbi R. Mendli [i.e., Mendel] of Rimonov[1] said before he departed: That after his departure he would make a great effort to help bring the time of redemption, and he would not enter the Garden of Eden until he could be certain of it. And it was so.[2]

And they showed him many different things [i.e., enticements], but he didn't agree to enter the Garden of Eden, because the end of days had not yet come. And they showed him the harp that played King David's melodies, may peace be upon him, and he followed the sweet voice of the harp and forgot all that was before him and entered into the midst of the Garden of Eden.

The Elder from Ujhel[3] [R. Moses Teitlebaum] said before his departure that he would not be tricked and for him the harp already didn't work, but they honored him with a sermon, and they said to him that when he was finished, the Redeemer would come and so he is still expounding....

And the Rav of Tzinz said, "Baruch"—his son R. Baruch of Ridnik—"do you think this is hyperbole?" No, [he answered,] this is true, he is still standing and expounding because there is above abundant wisdom and knowledge with no limit and they channel

(continued on page 185)

〜 **the past and the future are all one ...** The Rabbis teach, "There is no earlier or later in Torah" (Talmud, *Pesachim* 6b); also such is time in paradise. And so too often for the dying: time frames can be erased; last week, one hour ago, fifty years ago—all can become one in the same mix. It is as if the boundaries around time have faded and it is no longer linear. As companions to a dying person, we can also try to enter this timeless space and keep up with the thoughts that might drift by like passing clouds.

〜 **I will look after myself ...** This is a story of meaning making and of dying with purpose. He is determined not to be tricked into entering paradise (presumably from the purgatory of *Gehinnom*) until he has ensured the coming of the Messiah. He believes his work on earth is complete and he has done all that he can; now it is time to repair everything in the world-to-come so that nothing blocks the Messiah's arrival. This is his new hope. As we see with the dying, hope takes on new meaning every day. It is no longer a hope of living, but perhaps it is a hope of dying a painless death, or a quick death, or, as in this case, a death that can bring future meaning with it.

4 That is, "I won't be tricked."

〜 **he did not want [the doctor] ...** Similar to the Kotzker Rebbe, he sends the doctor away. Even though there might have been the possibility of extending life, he is ready to die and is clear that he is not interested in further curative or life-prolonging efforts. This can be a very challenging moment of decision for a dying person and for families. The moment when it is time to choose comfort over curative measures can be far from clear based on the many medical interventions possible, including trial studies that may or may not provide gain to the patient, though they may well advance medical understanding. There may also be times when it might be important to rule out depression before withdrawing all treatment. From the Yitav Lev we learn that if a person expresses readiness to die, it is likely for a reason, and it can be important to learn what is behind this decision so that there can be understanding and support up to the very end.

〜 See Insight Spark: Liminality.

wonderful innovations through him and he thinks that he is only beginning to explain, because there it is beyond time—**the past and the future are all one**. So, they tricked him as well, and they succeeded in getting him to enter.

"The Moharan of Ropshitz said, 'But they won't get me in with trickery.' And the Holy Rabbi of Tzinz said, 'They tricked even the Rav of Ropshitz, but when it comes to me, I think I will not be seduced.'"

And the Rav, master of the *Yitav Lev*, concluded, "With our numerous sins they even got the Rav of Tzinz to enter [the Garden of Eden], for they have many means, but me, **I will look after myself**."[4]

Before his departure they wanted to bring a great doctor. Perhaps there might be a hope, and **he did not want [the doctor]**, as he said, "If I have already repaired everything, I have nothing left to do in this world."

He was released on the sixth of Elul, 5643 (September 8, 1883).

[1] There was a famous debate between Rashi, a twelfth-century commenta-tor, and his grandson Rabbeinu Tam on the order in which the biblical texts are put into the tefillin boxes. The Talmud claims that the tefillin are kosher only if these texts are in the right order. There were thus two camps, and Rashi's became the dominant tradition.

[2] See note on "cover him with a sheet" in "The Ba'al Shem Tov."

[∿] **squeezed both his eyes tight ...** There is a sense of willfulness in this act, as the rabbi shuts out the world from his sight. We have read many stories now in *The Book of Departure* of rabbis trying to control the end and also of their *awareness* of impending death. In this story, rather than focusing on his squeezing his eyes tight in order to cause his death, it is the preparation for death and his awareness of it that can be a model for us. In his prayer and smile we experience his sense of mindfulness and of spiritual attunement, which emanates a sense of great peace and fulfillment in these final moments.

[∿] See Insight Sparks: Body and Soul; Liminality; The Timing of Death.

R. Yitzchak Yoel
of Kantikuziva

R. Yitzchak Yoel (1815–1875) lived in Ukraine. In 1869 he was arrested by the Russian government. Then in 1871 he was allowed to serve as rebbe of Yiktrinoslav under the watchful eyes of the police. A year later, he was freed entirely and permitted to resume a normal existence, which is when he became the *rav* in Kantikuziva.

R. Yitzchak Yoel of Kantikuziva, close to the time his soul left, called to his son and instructed his son to dress him in Rashi tefillin,[1] and he began to pray with a clear and level-headed mind and a smiling face. And after completing the *Shemoneh Esrei* prayer, he said, "My son, remove the tefillin from me, for there is no time."

After he had removed the tefillin from him, he [R. Yitzchak] stretched out his arms and legs and instructed them to cover his body with a sheet,[2] and he **squeezed both his eyes tight** and in one moment sent his soul to life eternal.

He was released on the twenty-fourth of Tammuz, 5635 (July 27, 1875).

◠ **a person should not fear death ...** In this, the last story in the collection—assuming that its being the last story is intentional—we are taught one clear lesson: not to fear death. As with almost all the *tzaddikim* whose end-of-life stories we have read, we are taught to welcome this event as a shedding of our physical bodies—their return to dust—so that our souls can experience their ultimate cleaving to God.

◠ **he closed himself in his special room ...** As in the opening story of the Ba'al Shem Tov, who took to his meditation room shortly before his departure, so here in our closing story we have a rebbe doing the same; we are taught that for some people it can be important to be alone before death, possibly reflecting on their lives and focusing their thoughts. Just as R. Shmuelke of Sasov quotes from Psalm 139 in asking his students to help him do his end-of-life review, so R. Gershon uses that psalm for the same purpose: taking stock and looking for any *teshuvah*, reconciliation and forgiveness, that he may need to do before his death.

1 That is, before he died.

◠ **see if a vexing way be in me ...** The rabbi is using this psalm to reflect on a lifetime of actions and any remaining sins. Another way to do this reflection is with the deathbed *Vidui*, a poetic final confession, and an important prayer that can be said with or for a dying person. This can be an enormously powerful moment and help create a sense of unity and a deep and strong connection between people.

2 Psalm 139:21–24. This is a fuller quoting from this biblical source than is found in the original, with the additional words in brackets. See the note on Psalm 139 in "R. Shmuelke of Sasov."

◠ **he had intense suffering ...** He accepts his suffering and teaches that we must accept it "with silence and prayer." This is in sharp contrast to the famous stories in the Talmud (*Berachot* 5b) where R. Yochanan asks R. Chiyya bar Abba if his sufferings are acceptable and he replies, "Neither they nor their reward." Here, R. Gershon is not concerned with reward, only that he show love and no grievances with God.

R. Gershon Chanoch Henech of Radzin

R. Gershon Chanoch Henech (Leiner) of Radzin (d. 1890) was also known as the Orchos Chayim. He was the grandson of R. Mordecai Yosef Leiner, the esteemed Izhbitzer Rebbe (1801–1854). He was a Torah scholar and a prolific writer, producing many manuscripts, including a compendium on *Seder Taharot* modeled after the Babylonian Talmud. Unfortunately, many of his writings have been lost. In the greater Jewish world, he is known for his mission to reinstate the use of *techelet*, the shade of blue referred to in the Torah (most famously in Numbers 15:38), by identifying the blood of the *chilazon* snail as its source.

A few weeks before the illness that killed R. Gershon Chanoch Henech of Radzin had occurred, he spoke at length on the matters of death, and said **a person should not fear death**, and other such teachings.

And when his illness overtook him and he was forced to take to his bed, **he closed himself in his special room** before he "lay down"[1] and they heard him reciting Psalms, "O Adonai, You know I hate those who hate You, [and loathe Your adversaries. With utter hatred I do hate them; they become my enemies. Search me, O God, and know my heart; probe me and know my mind. And **see if a vexing way be in me**,] and lead me on an everlasting path."[2]

And afterward he took to bed. And when the illness intensified and **he had intense suffering**, even though that was so, he didn't moan. And when they asked him why he didn't moan, that perhaps with groaning it might ease the pain, he answered and said, "The

(continued on page 191)

3   Talmud, *Berachot* 62a.

 ∿   See Insight Sparks: Meditation; Talking with God.

one who has grievances with the blessed Name groans, and whoever does not have grievances tolerates it all in silence and accepts the sufferings with love, like the 'tradition' relating to sufferings is with silence and prayer."[3]

He was released on the fourth of Tevet, 5651 (December 15, 1890).

At the beginning of the book of Exodus (2:23), the Israelites *groan*, the same verb, *aleph-nun-chet*, used in the story above: "And the Israelites groaned from the bondage and cried out, and their plea from the bondage rose up to God." That generation died in the desert before reaching the Promised Land. So too, for R. Gershon: the forty-second rebbe in this work; forty-two rebbes corresponding to the forty-two times Israel makes camp in its forty-year sojourn through the wilderness (Numbers 33). R. Gershon, namesake of a son of Moses, has left groaning behind for a long-gone generation. Here is a rabbi who, instead of reenacting the groaning of Exodus, fulfills one of the commands and promises of Deuteronomy: to love his God.

Talking with God

> As his soul came to rest he grabbed onto one of the hairs from the *peyot* on his head and said, "Master of the Universe, it is revealed and known before You that I did not benefit even by a hair's breadth from this world."
>
> —From the deathbed story of R. Israel of Ruzhin

Originating in a branch of Hasidic Judaism founded by the followers of R. Nachman of Breslov, *hitbodedut* is a spiritual practice that some Jews today have adopted. The term derives from a verb meaning "to isolate" or "to insulate" and translates in this instance as "self-reflection" or "meditation." Even more specifically, it points to a meditative practice that is linked to intimate communication with God—*talking* with God. For R. Nachman, it was a core practice of his life, at times even taking the form of self-isolation. Today, it is more likely to take a less extreme form in which people focus on their inner lives through meditation. It is, according to R. Nachman, "the highest level: it is greater than everything; it is *the* way to come closer to God, because it includes everything else" (*Likutei Moharan* II, 25). For Nachman, all of life is incorporated into *hitbodedut*. Specifically, this form of meditation involves intimate and almost "friendly" conversation with God.

Conclusion

In the course of studying these stories we have found that they lead us to five aspects of our human spiritual experience at the end of life: love, forgiveness and reconciliation, hope, gratitude, and meaning and legacy.

Love

The love people have with their partners, family members, and friends when fully realized can achieve the vision in Song of Songs, "Love as strong as death" (8:6).

In every phase of life, we journey with others: those who have gone before and those who stand with us now, and those who will come perhaps long after. We are part of a larger community (a Jewish community, a human community) that has known death and will continue to live after our bodies are gone; we are part of something stronger and larger than death. In story after story we have seen rebbes dying in the presence of students, friends, families—and God. In some of the stories love is at the center of the way in which their death holds meaning. For example, R. DovBaer of Mezritch speaks individually to each of his children and students, comforting them and helping them face the future. R. Israel of Polotzk, who is called by his friend to be buried alongside him, fulfills this calling with a deep sense of kindness. Similarly, R. Peretz of Przysucha dies together with his *rav*, and they are buried together. R. Yitzchak Meir's final act is to call his grandson to his side to teach him. All of these rabbis' deaths were guided and made whole by a strong and deep loving connection.

Forgiveness and Reconciliation

Here is a peace that is achieved by working through the tangles of our lives with those living and those who have come before us as well, and also for some, with God, and with the possibility of arriving at the gracious moment in the Priestly Blessing, "May God lift up God's face unto you and give you peace" (Numbers 6:24–27).

There is an opportunity for some people at the end of life to become more healed, more whole, than ever before by addressing regrets and unfinished business, mending relationships, and speaking with people about things that should be laid to rest, and for some, mending their relationship with God as well. In the story of R. Nachman of Breslov, he not only heals those near to him, but he also prepares to heal those waiting in the world-to-come. R. Eliezer said, "Repent one day before your death" (*Mishnah Avot* 2:10). His disciples asked him, "Does then one know on what day he will die?" "All the more reason he should repent today, lest he die tomorrow" (Talmud, *Shabbat* 153a).

In these stories we witness not final deathbed confessions as we understand them today, but deathbed scenes very similar to Jacob's—a gathering together of those close to the one dying, and a blessing or expression of values. The Rabbis of the Mishnah enticed us into confession by saying that "all who confess have a place in the world-to-come" (*Mishnah Sanhedrin* 6:2). Centuries later the Rabbis of the Talmud were even more commanding in their statement: "If one falls ill and his life is in danger, he is told, 'Make confession.' For all who are sentenced to death make confession" (Talmud, *Shabbat* 32a). The rabbis in the stories of *The Book of Departure* are special insofar as their deaths are understood to result in atonement for their whole generation. R. Avraham Yehoshua Heschel, the Apter Rebbe, like R. Nachman, is bartering with his death for the souls of people, atonement for his own life and for all the people of his community who have gone before him. R. Naftali Chaim makes it clear that he is not in need of atonement, for he has not benefited in any way from the physical world; his conscience is clear.

Toward the very end of a life, when it is welcomed by patients, we can offer to recite a final *Vidui*, the Jewish end-of-life confession, as a way to help them find their own sense of peace before dying. Though the formal *Vidui* can be a bit challenging to some people—"May my death be atonement for all the errors, iniquities, and willful sins that I have erred, sinned, and transgressed before You"—there are alternative translations that may bring comfort to the dying and those close to them.

Hope

Hope can be redefined or redirected in facing death to be about each day, things that will happen in the world beyond one's lifetime, or ideas about an afterlife. "Weeping may endure for a night, but joy comes in the morning" (Psalm 30:6).

Prominent Modern Orthodox authority Maurice Lamm tell us, "Judaism says we may not take away [a] person's ecstatic hope.... Without lying, without pandering, a caregiver must translate that hope into a more realistic one, perhaps hope to live without pain, a hope that her dreams for her family may well be realized, and surely a hope that God will care for her."[9]

When most of us think of hope, we think of life and light, but for many of the dying what hope means is having their families near as they die, knowing that their families are all right with their death, or being assured that they will be free of pain, be kept clean, or have human touch. They no longer have hope that they will live, because they know that specific hope in life will no longer be realized. Some see God, and their hope is to be able to join God for eternity; others find hope in a life review that reminds them of the eternality of their actions, of what they have done in their lives. When R. Aaron of Zhitomir is dying and his students begin to cry, he says to them, "Why are you weeping? The ending of all people is to die." He expresses the reality of the situation, he expresses where his hope lies, and he invites them to support him in his journey—which one day will be theirs as well.

R. Menachem Mendel of Vitebsk tells people to stop blocking his view because "God is standing above me." God, not life, is his future—it is where his hope now lies. R. Zev of Zhitomir expresses very real hope in the leaders that will come after him. For some people, their hope lies with their children and grandchildren—in future lives that will carry on after their own life is gone.

Gratitude

Gratitude may rise up in a person who has drunk fully of life and experienced blessing. This is embodied in the morning prayer, "I thank You, God, living and eternal One, for returning my soul into my body with compassion; my faith is great." And with the arrival of death, that trust and fullness are not diminished.

With these words from the morning service, many Jews begin the day—an immediate expression of gratitude for life, for the soul that God has placed within them, and for God's eternal faithfulness. So important is this posture for daily living that, according to tradition, it is said as feet hit the ground from bed, even before washing.

There are a number of ways of saying the word "gratitude" in Hebrew. Perhaps the most common and certainly the simplest is *hodayah*, "thanks." But also interesting are the idioms *hachzakat tovah*, "holding on to or grasping the good," and *hakarat tovah*, "recognizing the good." Is that not what gratitude is—recognizing the good that is in our lives and holding it close to us? Torah tells us how to do this in Deuteronomy 30:14, "For this thing is very close to you, in your mouth and on your heart, to do it."

In the story of R. Zusha of Plotzk, just before he dies he quotes, "I will arise at midnight to thank you" (Psalm 119:62), as if he were saying, "I can hardly wait to arise in the morning so that I can give thanks for Your presence in the world." Indeed, all of Psalm 119, the longest psalm in the Bible, is an expression of the depth to which the psalmist loves God, appreciates God, and is grateful for the great gifts God has bestowed on humankind—certainly primary among those gifts is Torah. Indeed, almost every one of the twenty-two stanzas of the psalm—one for each letter of the Hebrew alphabet—contains a synonym of some kind for Torah.

R. DovBaer of Mezritch expresses his gratitude with a joy-filled heart that affirms his trust in God. R. Aaron of Staroselye dances and celebrates life up until his final moments. R. Shmuelke of Sasov sings out his praise of God. Some people simply exude a sense of fullness and thankfulness as they near death and can share the peace that comes with this emotion with those around them.

Meaning and Legacy

The attributes of meaning and legacy can be retained so that even in the face of illness and physical weakness, people feel the worth and fortitude of their beliefs, recognize the power of the life they have lived, and see the results of their life that will continue on in the world. "May the favor of Adonai, our God, be upon us, and let the work of our hands be established" (Psalm 90:17).

Of all the stories in *The Book of Departure*, perhaps none brings home the message of meaning and legacy as does the story of Menachem Mendel of Vitebsk. Here we see one rebbe as both patient and teacher: "He was so wasted and thin that he no longer seemed human. Still, his mind was strong, his teaching clear, and he chose his words with a settled mind and sparkling logic, until the final chapter." He retained his sense of purpose *and* was understood as a great teacher to the very end.

"In my forty years as a rabbi," writes R. Harold Kushner, "I have tended to many people in the last moments of their lives. Most of them were not afraid of dying. Some were old and felt they had lived long, satisfying lives. Others were so sick and in such pain that only death would release them. The people who had the most trouble with death were those who felt that they had never done anything worthwhile in their lives, and if God would only give them another two or three years, maybe they would finally get it right. It was not death that frightened them; it was insignificance, the fear that they would die and leave no mark on the world."[10]

The writing and delivery of an ethical will can be an important part of the dying and grieving process and affirm a person's legacy. Recall the following story: "When he was approaching his time to depart from this world, R. Elimelech of Lizhensk placed his hands on the heads of his students and to four of them to whom he was closest he distributed aspects of his soul." Aspects of his very *soul*! This end-of-life narrative theology is so much more than the telling of stories and relaying of values; it is the way in which dying people can distribute their souls to ensuing generations. Those stories and their attendant values get repeated; they get processed by the family over the generations and in time gain a life of their own, so that perhaps a time comes when the person is no longer remembered but his or her values live on.

What a powerful aspect of the Jewish ethos is this sense of generation—of one generation leaving an ethical, intellectual, spiritual legacy for those who follow. So many of the stories that comprise *The Book of Departure* are filled with what one generation leaves to the next. R. Shneur Zalman of Liadi is writing and teaching his grandson right up until his final moments of life; R. Rafael of Bershad dies rather than have a life of truth be marred with a lie; R. Naftali of Ropshitz will only pray at the end of life and not speak, for he no longer has the strength of mind to speak with the integrity that he had throughout his life. All are models of people who left incredible ethical legacies through their teachings and actions.

Acknowledgments

We would like to thank Rabbi Ebn Leader, who introduced us to *The Book of Departure*; Rabbi Arthur Green, who shared his valuable time with us; and Rabbi Shayna Rhodes, Rev. Mary Martha Thiel, Simchah Rafael, and Rabbi Herman Blumberg. We thank Stuart M. Matlins, publisher; Emily Wichland, vice president of Editorial & Production; and the team at Jewish Lights. We are also grateful to Hebrew College, Hebrew SeniorLife, and Hebrew SeniorLife Hospice Care, the settings where much of the learning about pastoral care that undergirds this work has taken place. Most of all, we are grateful to our patients and the loving families and friends who have helped care for them and welcomed us into their lives.

The Characteristics of Active Dying

To help those caring for people at the end of life, we include a set of behaviors and symptoms to anticipate as a person moves into the category that healthcare providers refer to as "active dying." The following has been adapted from a fuller accounting found on WebMD:[11]

One to two weeks prior to death, a person may be or become bed-bound and experience:

- Increased pain, which the healthcare professionals can manage
- Changes in blood pressure, heart rate, and respiratory rate, which a nurse will attempt to manage, as it takes stress off the person
- Continued loss of appetite and thirst and difficulty taking medications by mouth
- Decline in bowel and bladder output
- Changes in sleep-wake patterns
- Temperature fluctuations that may leave the skin cool, feverish feeling, moist, or pale
- Constant fatigue
- The appearance of what books have called a "death rattle," which is actually congested breathing caused by the buildup of secretions at the back of the throat; this is not painful to the person and can be managed to some degree, though it can be *very* distressing for loved ones.
- Disorientation or seeing and talking to people who don't appear to be there to others but who may well seem to be there to the dying person. These visions can be comforting, so it's best not to try convincing the person that they aren't real. Doing so with

someone who is pleasantly confused can make the person agitated and combative.

When death is just days or hours away:

- The person may no longer want food or drink.
- There may be little or no bladder or bowel activity.
- Pain may increase further and can be managed.
- Eyes may tear or become glazed.
- If not already unconscious, the dying person may drift in and out of consciousness. Keep talking to your loved one and holding his or her hand because the person probably can still hear and feel— hearing is the last of the senses to go.
- Pulse and heartbeat may become irregular or difficult to detect.
- Body temperature will drop, and the skin of the knees, feet, and hands will become a mottled bluish purple. Once the mottling starts, death often occurs within twenty-four hours.
- Toward the very end the person may experience what doctors call terminal delirium: heightened activity and confusion often accompanied by hallucinations, so distressful to the person that he or she may cry out, strike out, or even try to climb out of bed. Since the person could hurt him- or herself, it's important that a healthcare provider try to stop the delirium with medications or other nondrug interventions.
- Breathing, punctuated by gasping starts and stops, will slow until it stops entirely. This is difficult to witness, but the dying person is not in pain from it. His or her body is simply shutting down. Know that he or she is about to die. Try to breathe deeply, releasing any fear you may have on your exhale, and bring love and compassion to the person you're with.

Notes

1. Martin Buber, *Tales of the Hasidim* (New York: Schocken Books, 1975), 5.
2. Simcha Paull Raphael, *Jewish Views of the Afterlife* (Lanham, MD: Rowman & Littlefield Publishers, 2009), 13.
3. Shlomo Yaffe and Yanki Tauber, "What Happens after We Die?," Chabad.org, www.chabad.org/library/article_cdo/aid/282508/jewish/What-Happens-After-We-Die.htm.
4. Aryeh Kaplan, *The Handbook of Jewish Thought*, vol. 2 (Brooklyn: Moznaim Publishing, 1992), 335–39.
5. Nehemia Polen, "Miriam's Dance: Radical Egalitarianism in Hasidic Thought," *Modern Judaism* 12 (1992): 1–21.
6. Rami Shapiro, *Hasidic Tales: Annotated and Explained* (Woodstock, VT: SkyLight Paths Publishing, 2004), xxi.
7. Maurice Lamm, *The Jewish Way in Death and Mourning* (Middle Village, NY: Jonathan David Publishers, 2000), 3.
8. Raphael, *Jewish Views of the Afterlife*, 140.
9. www.centerforjewishendoflifecare.org/facilitating-conversations/religious-leaders/what-do-successful-conversations-sound-like.
10. Harold S. Kushner, *Living a Life That Matters* (New York: Knopf, 2001), 6.
19. "Journey's End: Active Dying," WebMD, www.webmd.com/palliative-care/journeys-end-active-dying.

Glossary

Adar: Hebrew month roughly corresponding to February–March. In leap years there are two Adars; Adar I is added to make the regular Adar into Adar II.

Av: Hebrew month roughly corresponding to July–August.

Besht: Acronym for the *Ba'al Shem Tov* ("The Master of the Good Name [of God]"), referring to R. Israel ben Eliezer (1698–1760), the leader around whose teaching Hasidism is centered.

Chabad: Chabad Hasidism was founded by R. Shneur Zalman of Liadi (1745–1812). The word "Chabad" is an acronym for the three Hebrew words *Chochmah* (Wisdom), *Binah* (Understanding), and *Da'at* (Knowledge), three of the ten mystical attributes through which God reveals Godself and which form the intellectual foundations of Chabad. Chabad is well known for its outreach, particularly toward nonpracticing Jews.

chesed: Hebrew word meaning "loving-kindness," and one of the ten mystical attributes (*sefirot*), or emanations, through which God reveals Godself.

Cheshvan: Hebrew month roughly corresponding to October–November.

chevra kadisha, chevraya kadisha: A Jewish burial society (literally, "holy society") of community volunteers who do the traditional washing, dressing, and blessing of the body of the deceased.

derash, drash: An interpretation of text, usually Scripture, and it can refer to a short interpretation that is delivered as part of a religious service.

deveikut: Hebrew word literally meaning the state of "cleaving" or "clinging to." *Deveikut* represents a spiritually ideal state in which one's soul cleaves directly with God. It may also refer to a meditative state achieved during prayer, study, or when performing any of the commandments (Hebrew, *mitzvot*) identified in the Torah. In Torah, the root of the word *deveikut* is used in Genesis to describe the relationship between husband and wife, and in Deuteronomy Moses uses the same verb to describe how Israel must hold on to God.

Elul: Hebrew month roughly corresponding to August–September.

etrog: A fruit similar to a lemon but more aromatic and generally slightly larger; it is one of four fruits and trees of the Land of Israel mentioned in the Torah as part of the celebration of the holiday of Sukkot.

***Gehinnom*, Gehenna:** Originally described in 2 Chronicles 28:3 as the place where children were sacrificed to the god Moloch. The Bible refers to *Gei ven Hinnom* (literally, "the valley of the son of Hinnom"), a place south of Jerusalem. Tradition has it that the very righteous go directly to the Garden of Eden when they die, while the average person's soul goes to *Gehinnom* (in English, Gehenna), where it is cleansed over a period of twelve months. After that, the soul returns to God, taking its place in the *olam haba*, the world-to-come.

***goses*:** A person who is actively dying and is thought to be in the final minutes, hours, or at most three days of life.

***hakafot*:** Hebrew word meaning "circuits," and describing a part of the prayer services on Sukkot and Simchat Torah when people walk or dance around in a circle. On the festival of Sukkot people walk in a circle carrying their *lulav* and *etrog* and making blessings. On Simchat Torah people generally walk or dance with singing and spirit around the perimeter of the synagogue with some people in the middle dancing with the Torah scrolls. The circle, in many traditions, represents unity, perfection, and community and is a concept very close to the hearts of Hasidim.

halachic: Adjective form of the Hebrew word *halachah*, meaning "law," referring to a large body of work that derives from Scripture.

***Hallel*:** *Hallel* is a special service of joy and thanksgiving chanted after the morning *Shemoneh Esrei* prayer (see below), and consists of Psalms 113–18 recited as a unit. The *Hallel* service is included on joyous occasions, specifically including Passover, Shavuot, Sukkot, Hanukkah, and Rosh Hodesh (beginning of the new month).

***Hashem*:** Literally, "the Name"; a metaphorical way of referring to God.

Hasidism: A popular and democratizing movement within Judaism that arose in the mid-seventeenth century in Eastern Europe; see the section entitled "What Is Hasidism?" in the introduction to this book.

***Hasidut*:** The teachings and practices of Hasidic Judaism; literally, "piety."

***histalkut*:** Hebrew word meaning "departure." For a full discussion of this word, see "Insight Spark: The Language of Death."

***hitbodedut*:** A term that derives from a verb meaning "to isolate" or "to insulate" and is often used to express a practice of self-reflection or meditation; it points to a meditative practice that is linked to intimate communication with God—*talking* with God.

hitbonenut: Related to *hitbodedut* (above), an in-depth form of meditation that may lead one to higher levels of cleaving to God as opposed to communicating with God through *hitbodedut*.

Hoshanah Rabbah: A holiday observed on the seventh day of the Jewish holiday of Sukkot; the name literally translates as "the Great Hoshanah" or "the Great Supplication." Hoshanah Rabbah is known as the last of the Days of Judgment that began on Rosh Hashanah. During the synagogue service that marks this day, seven circuits (see ***hakafot***) are made by the worshipers with their *lulav* and *etrog*, while the congregation recites *Hoshanot* (literally, "Save! I pray!"), a series of poetical prayers.

Iyar: Hebrew month roughly corresponding to April–May.

Kabbalah: Derived from the Hebrew root meaning "to receive," the name "Kabbalah," referring to a mystical text, implies "received wisdom" concerning God and the universe. Kabbalah first emerged in twelfth- to thirteenth-century France and Spain, being understood as available only to a privileged few, and then reemerged in sixteenth-century Palestine. It was popularized in Hasidic Judaism during the eighteenth century and has continued to be a primary area of study and practice.

kavanah **(pl.** *kavanot***):** Literally, "intention." *Kavanah* is often described as the direction of the heart or spiritual intention.

Kislev: Hebrew month roughly corresponding to November–December.

kohen **(pl.** *kohanim***):** Pronounced ko-HEYN; the *kohanim* were the priestly class in biblical times. They were descendants of Moses's brother Aaron and were members of the Levite tribe, one of the twelve tribes of Israel.

lulav: A "bouquet" of three of the four species identified in Leviticus as part of the Sukkot ritual: a closed date palm frond (*lulav*), a cutting from a myrtle bush (*hadas*), and a twig from a willow tree (*aravah*). Collectively it is referred to as a *lulav*.

met/metah: The body of a dead person.

mezuzah (pl. mezuzot): A case containing a piece of parchment on which are written the verses 6:4–9 and 11:13–21 from the book of Deuteronomy. These verses comprise the *Shema* prayer. The mezuzah is affixed to the right side (as one enters the house or room) of a door frame in order to fulfill the commandment "You shall inscribe them on the doorposts of your house and on your gates" (Deuteronomy 6:9).

Midrash: A body of interpretations of biblical texts and homiletic stories that were taught and collected beginning in the post-Temple period. Midrashim were written down at different times, over a period of almost a thousand years, largely from 300–1200 CE. Midrash evolved as a method of filling in gaps left in the biblical narrative and resolving problems in understanding difficult passages of text.

Mishnah: The Mishnah, a foundational work of Jewish law, is a six-volume redaction of Jewish oral traditions. Discussed, argued, and compiled by the Rabbis beginning at the very onset of the Common Era, the Mishnah was redacted by Rabbi Yehudah haNasi (d. ca. 217 CE).

Mishneh Torah: The fourteen-volume medieval work of Moses Maimonides that details all of Jewish observance.

mitnagdim: The rapid rise of Hasidism in Eastern Europe and Russia gave rise in the mid-1700s to an informal movement of largely Lithuanian Jews who were vehemently opposed to Hasidism. By the mid-1800s these *mitnagdim* (Hebrew for "opponents") made their peace with the Hasidim.

mitzvah (pl. mitzvot): Literally, "commandment." Any of the 613 laws Jews are expected to observe as enumerated in the Torah and explicated in the Mishnah and Talmud. For many Jews the term has also come to simply mean "a good deed."

***niggun* (pl. *niggunim*):** A wordless melody, usually repeated multiple times, that is central to Hasidic prayer and intended to stir one's soul and help induce *kavanah*.

Nisan: Hebrew month roughly corresponding to March–April.

Pale of Settlement: The contiguous areas of Poland, Ukraine, Lithuania, and Belorussia where Jews were confined to live, largely during the period 1791–1917.

***parashah* (n.), *parashat* (adj.), *parshiyot* (pl.):** Literally, "a section" of the Torah. The Torah is read weekly in Jewish tradition, on Mondays, Thursdays, and Saturdays. All told, there are fifty-four *parshiyot*, one for each week of the year, so that in the course of a year, we read the entire Torah; in non-leap years certain *parshiyot* are combined.

petirah: Hebrew word meaning "departure" or "release." For a full discussion of this word, see "Insight Spark: The Language of Death."

pogrom: Russian word for the physical attacks against Jews in Russia, specifically during the period 1881–1921.

R., Rebbe, Rav, Rabbeinu: All are forms of the title "Rabbi." *Rabbeinu* (literally, "our Rabbi") has special significance, as it generally refers to Moses.

rebbetzin: The wife of the rabbi. The rabbi's wife has a legendary role in the life of the rabbi and her family, as well as in the life of the community. Particularly in the realm of women's laws and practices, she is expected to be expert and will often advise, especially when the petitioner may not want to talk directly to the rabbi.

Ribbono shel Olam: Literally, "Master of the Universe"; a reference to God.

Rosh Hodesh: The first day of a lunar month. (There are months in which it can last for two days.)

Rosh Hashanah: The first day of the Jewish New Year, and one of the most significant days in the Jewish calendar. In Jewish religious practice, it is a time of celebration and confession of personal and communal sins.

seder: Literally, "order," the seder is the ritualized (i.e., "ordered") meal observed in the home on the first two evenings of Passover and during which symbolic foods are eaten and stories of the Exodus are told, based on passages from Torah and the tradition.

Shabbat, Shabbos: The seventh day; the Sabbath. For traditional Jews this day runs from one hour before sundown on Friday to when three stars are visible in the sky on Saturday evening. It is a day when people abstain from creative work and engage in rest and prayer. Shabbat is often a time when friends and family gather over meals and conclude with prayer and song.

Shechinah: A name for God that is understood to be the presence of God that dwells among people and is thought to be a feminine aspect of God.

Shema: A central prayer in Jewish practice that repeats the words of Deuteronomy 6:4, "Hear, O Israel, Adonai is our God, Adonai is One." The prayer then continues with verses 5–9, and together they are referred to as the first paragraph of the *Shema*.

Shemoneh Esrei: Literally, "eighteen," a number used as one of the names of the core of every Jewish prayer service; the service is also called the *Tefilah* (the Prayer; the Worship) or the *Amidah* (the Standing). Traditionally, the weekday *Shemoneh Esrei* comprises eighteen prayers, which are generally praises of or supplications to God; on Shabbat and holidays the structure of the prayer is altered.

Shevat: Hebrew month roughly corresponding to January–February.

shomer: Literally, "guardian." The term *shomer* takes on a variety of meanings under Jewish law, but for the purposes of this book the *shomer* is a person who accepts the responsibility for staying with a dead person from as soon after physical death as possible until others assume that role at the funeral and burial itself. The *shomer* generally fulfills this mitzvah also by reciting or studying scriptural passages, particularly psalms, and especially Psalms 23 and 91.

siddur: A prayer book.

simchah: A joyous event.

Sivan: Hebrew month roughly corresponding to May–June.

Sukkot: One of the three formal Pilgrimage Festivals identified in the book of Exodus. Sukkot, a seven-day (eight in the Diaspora) observance, is called in English the "Feast of Tabernacles" and sometimes the "Feast of the Ingathering." The observance of Sukkot derives from the Bible and has a double significance: one is agricultural in nature, marking the end of the agricultural year in Israel; the more religious significance is in commemorating the wandering in the desert after the Exodus, during which time people lived in temporary huts (Hebrew, *sukkot*) in the desert.

tallit: A fringed shawl worn by Jews in morning prayer services. The tallit has special twined and knotted fringes known as *tzitzit* attached to its four corners. In biblical times it is assumed that people attached the *tzitzit* to the garment they were wearing; some scholars believe that by 1000 CE a practice had evolved where the *tzitzit* became attached to a separate garment, as is worn today. The command to wear *tzitzit* can be found in Numbers 15:38–41: "Speak to the Israelites and say to them that they should make them a fringe on the corners of their garments for their generations ... and you shall see it and recall all Adonai's commandments and you shall do them."

Talmud: Edited and compiled over hundreds of years, ending ca. 500 CE, the Talmud is an organized collection of what is known as Oral Law: teachings, opinions, and stories on a variety of subjects, including Jewish law, Jewish ethics, philosophy, customs, history, lore, and many other topics. The Babylonian Talmud (there was also a Talmud created in Jerusalem, though the Babylonian has become by far the dominant book) comprises sixty-three tractates and in the standard edition is over sixty-two hundred pages long. It is written in Aramaic and Hebrew and is the basis for all codes of Jewish law.

Tammuz: Hebrew month roughly corresponding to June–July.

Tanya: Written by Shneur Zalman of Liadi, the *Tanya* is the main work of the Chabad philosophy and its approach to Hasidic mysticism.

tefillin: Small, cube-shaped black boxes that are attached to the head and arm during morning prayers and containing four passages from Scripture.

Tevet: Hebrew month roughly corresponding to December–January.

Tishrei: Hebrew month roughly corresponding to September–October.

Torah: The first section of the Hebrew Bible consisting of the Five Books of Moses: Genesis, Exodus, Leviticus, Numbers, and Deuteronomy.

***tzaddik* (pl. *tzaddikim*):** A righteous one (see the section entitled "What Is a *Tzaddik*?" in the introduction to this book).

unification: Unifications are a specific form of meditation in kabbalistic mysticism based on techniques developed by Isaac Luria (1534–1572). There were specific practices Luria gave to his followers based on their individual spiritual needs.

***Vidui*:** A confessional prayer recited several times on Yom Kippur (the Day of Atonement); also traditionally recited before one dies.

world-to-come: Literal translation of the Hebrew term *olam haba*, indicating the Jewish afterlife.

***yahrzeit*:** The anniversary of a death which is primarily observed for deceased parents, a *yahrzeit* is marked by reciting a Kaddish prayer and lighting a twenty-four-hour memorial candle.

Yehudah haNasi: Second-century-CE rabbi and redactor of the Mishnah.

yeshivah: A Jewish institution of study and learning, traditionally devoting study mainly to Torah and Talmud.

***Zohar*:** A complex, multivolume work foundational in the literature of Jewish mystical thought (see **Kabbalah**). The *Zohar* comprises commentary on the mystical aspects of Torah and scriptural interpretations, as well as material on the study of mysticism.

Suggestions for Further Reading

Albeck, Hanoch. *Mavo la-Mishnah*. Jerusalem: Bialik Institute and Dvir Co. Tel Aviv, 1959.

Berger, Michael S. *Rabbinic Authority*. Oxford: Oxford University Press, 1998.

Brenner, Daniel S., Tsvi Blanchard, Joseph J. Fins, and Bradley Hirschfield. *Embracing Life and Facing Death: A Jewish Guide to Palliative Care*. New York: CLAL—The National Jewish Center for Learning and Leadership, 2002.

Buber, Martin. *Tales of the Hasidim*. New York: Schocken Books, 1947, 1975.

Butler, Katy. *Knocking on Heaven's Door*. New York: Scribner, 2013.

Cohen, Martin S., ed. *The Observant Life*. New York: The Rabbinic Assembly, 2012.

Eilberg, Amy. "Jewish Principles of Care for the Dying." *The Outstretched Arm* (Winter 2001): 1.

Elior, Rachel. "Early Forms of Jewish Mysticism." In *The Cambridge History of Judaism*, vol. 4, edited by Steven T. Katz, 749–91. Cambridge: Cambridge University Press, 2006.

Fishbane, Michael. *The Kiss of God: Spiritual and Mystical Death in Judaism*. Seattle: University of Washington Press, 1994.

Fox, Joseph. *Menachem Mendel of Kotzk: A Biographical Study of the Chasidic Master*. New York: Bash Publications, 1988.

Gawande, Atul. *Being Mortal: Medicine and What Matters in the End*. New York: Metropolitan Books, 2014.

Gillman, Neil. *Believing and Its Tensions: A Personal Conversation about God, Torah, Suffering and Death in Jewish Thought*. Woodstock, VT: Jewish Lights Publishing, 2013.

—— *The Death of Death: Resurrection and Immortality in Jewish Thought*. Woodstock, VT: Jewish Lights Publishing, 2000.

——. *Traces of God: Seeing God in Torah, History and Everyday Life*. Woodstock, VT: Jewish Lights Publishing, 2008.

Ginzberg, Louis. *The Legends of the Jews*. 7 vols. Translated by Paul Rudin. Philadelphia: The Jewish Publication Society of America, 1911.

Glatt, Aaron. *Visiting the Sick: A Halachic and Medical Guide with Down-to-Earth Advice.* Brooklyn: Mesorah Publications, 2006.

Goodman, Ellen. *The Conversation Project.* n.d. http://theconversationproject.org.

Green, Arthur. *Tormented Master: The Life and Spiritual Quest of Rabbi Nahman of Bratslav.* Woodstock, VT: Jewish Lights Publishing, 1992.

Halifax, Joan. *Being with Dying: Cultivating Compassion and Fearlessness in the Presence of Death.* Boston: Shambhala Publications, 2008.

Horodezky, Samuel Abba. *Ha-Hasidut veha-Hasidim.* Vol. 4. Berlin: Dewir, 1922.

Jacobs, Louis. *The Jewish Religion: A Companion.* New York: Oxford University Press, 1995.

Kaminetzy, Yosef Y. *Days in Chabad: Historic Events in the Dynasty of Chabad-Lubavitch.* Brooklyn: Merkos Linyonei Chinuch, 2002.

Kaplan, Aryeh. *The Handbook of Jewish Thought.* Vol. 2. Brooklyn: Moznaim Publishing, 1992.

Kushner, Harold S. *The Jewish Way in Death and Mourning.* Middle Village, NY: Jonathan David Publishers, 2000.

———. *Living a Life That Matters.* New York: Knopf, 2001.

Levine, Aaron. *How to Perform the Great Mitzva of Bikkur Cholim.* Willowdale, Ont: Zichron Meir Publications, 1987.

Matt, Daniel C. *The Zohar: Pritzker Edition.* 10 vols. Stanford, CA: Stanford University Press, 2004–2016.

Mintz, Benjamin. *Sefer haHistalkut.* Limudei Yahedut v'Ruach: Daat, 1930. www.daat.ac.il/daat/history/hasidut/sefer-2.htm.

———. *Sefer haHistalkut.* Tel Aviv: Ketuvim, 1930.

Moss, Steven A. *The Attitude toward Sickness, Dying and Death as Expressed in the Liturgical Works "Maavor Yabok" and "Sefer Hahayiim."* Thesis submitted in partial fulfillment of requirements for the master of arts in Hebrew literature degree and ordination, Hebrew Union College–Jewish Institute of Religion, New York (available at www.jewish-funerals.org/attitude-toward-sickness-dying-and-death-expressed-liturgical-works-maavor-yabok-and-sefer-hahayiim-0), 1974.

Noson, Nathan of Breslov, a.k.a. Reb Noson, a.k.a. David Sternhartz. *Tzaddik: A Portrait of Rabbi Nachman.* Translated by Avraham Greenbaum. Lakewood, NJ: Breslov Research Institute, 1987.

Paasche-Orlow, Sara, and Mary Martha Thiel. "Seven Basic Spiritual/Religious Issues and Corresponding Approaches to Pastoral Care." Boston: Hebrew

SeniorLife Spiritual Assessment Tool, Department of Religious and Chaplaincy Services, n.d.

Polen, Nehemia. "Miriam's Dance: Radical Egalitarianism in Hasidic Thought." *Modern Judaism* 12 (1992): 1–21.

Raphael, Simcha Paull. *Jewish Views of the Afterlife*. Lanham, MD: Rowman and Littlefield Publishers, 2009.

Riemer, Jack. *Jewish Insights on Death and Mourning*. Syracuse, NY: Syracuse University Press, 1995.

Riemer, Jack, and Nathaniel Stampfer. *Ethical Wills and How to Prepare Them: A Guide to Sharing Your Values from Generation to Generation*. Woodstock, VT: Jewish Lights Publishing, 2015.

Shapira, Kalonymus Kalman. *Conscious Community: A Guide to Inner Work*. Translated by Andrea Cohen-Kiener. Lanham, MD: Rowman and Littlefield Publishers, 1996.

Shapiro, Rami. *Hasidic Tales: Annotated & Explained*. Woodstock, VT: SkyLight Paths Publishing, 2004.

Spitz, Elie Kaplan. *Does the Soul Survive? A Jewish Journey to Afterlife, Past Lives and Living with Purpose*. 2nd ed. Woodstock, VT: Jewish Lights Publishing, 2015.

Tighe, Elizabeth, et al. *American Jewish Population Estimates 2012*. Waltham, MA: Brandeis University Steinhardt Social Research Institute, 2013.

Veale, Sarah. "The Lurianic Revolution in Kabbalah: Reinterpreting Jewish Mysticism, Responding to Cultural Trends." *Academia.edu*. January 28, 2014.

Wertheim, Aaron. *Law and Custom in Hasidism*. Hoboken, NJ: Ktav Publishing House, 1992.

Zalman, of Liady, Shneuer. *Igrois Koidesh: Admur Hazoken, Admur Ha'Emtz'ee, Admur Hatzemach Tzedek*. Brooklyn: "Kehot" Publication Society, 1987.

Index of Rabbis in
The Book of Departure

Grief / Healing

Does the Soul Survive? 2nd Edition: A Jewish Journey to Belief in Afterlife, Past Lives & Living with Purpose
By Rabbi Elie Kaplan Spitz; Foreword by Brian L. Weiss, MD
A skeptic turned believer recounts his quest to uncover the Jewish tradition's answers about what happens to our souls after death, looking squarely at both sides of the issues. 6 x 9, 288 pp, Quality PB, 978-1-58023-818-2 **$18.99**

Ethical Wills & How to Prepare Them: A Guide to Sharing Your Values from Generation to Generation *Edited by Rabbi Jack Riemer and Dr. Nathaniel Stampfer; Foreword by Rabbi Harold S. Kushner* 6 x 9, 272 pp, Quality PB, 978-1-58023-827-4 **$18.99**

Facing Illness, Finding God: How Judaism Can Help You and Caregivers Cope When Body or Spirit Fails *By Rabbi Joseph B. Meszler*
6 x 9, 208 pp, Quality PB, 978-1-58023-423-8 **$16.99**

Grief in Our Seasons: A Mourner's Kaddish Companion *By Rabbi Kerry M. Olitzky*
4½ x 6½, 448 pp, Quality PB, 978-1-879045-55-2 **$18.99**

Healing and the Jewish Imagination: Spiritual and Practical Perspectives on Judaism and Health *Edited by Rabbi William Cutter, PhD*
6 x 9, 240 pp, Quality PB, 978-1-58023-373-6 **$19.99**

Healing and the Jewish Imagination: Spiritual and Practical Perspectives on Judaism and Health *Edited by Rabbi William Cutter, PhD*
6 x 9, 240 pp, Quality PB, 978-1-58023-373-6 **$19.99**

Healing from Despair: Choosing Wholeness in a Broken World
By Rabbi Elie Kaplan Spitz with Erica Shapiro Taylor; Foreword by Abraham J. Twerski, MD
5½ x 8½, 208 pp, Quality PB, 978-1-58023-436-8 **$16.99**

The Jewish Book of Grief and Healing: A Spiritual Companion for Mourning
Edited by Stuart M. Matlins and the Editors at Jewish Lights; Preface by Rabbi Anne Brener, LCSW; Foreword by Dr. Ron Wolfson 6 x 9, 176 pp, Quality PB, 978-1-58023-852-6 **$16.99**

Judaism and Health: A Handbook of Practical, Professional and Scholarly Resources *Edited by Jeff Levin, PhD, MPH, and Michele F. Prince, LCSW, MAJCS
Foreword by Rabbi Elliot N. Dorff, PhD* 6 x 9, 448 pp, HC, 978-1-58023-714-7 **$50.00**

Judaism's Ten Best Ideas: A Brief Guide for Seekers
By Rabbi Arthur Green 4½ x 6½, 112 pp, Quality PB, 978-1-58023-803-8 **$9.99**

Midrash & Medicine: Healing Body and Soul in the Jewish Interpretive Tradition
Edited by Rabbi William Cutter, PhD; Foreword by Michele F. Prince, LCSW, MAJCS
6 x 9, 352 pp, Quality PB, 978-1-58023-484-9 **$21.99**

Mourning & Mitzvah, 2nd Edition: A Guided Journal for Walking the Mourner's Path through Grief to Healing *By Rabbi Anne Brener, LCSW*
7½ x 9, 304 pp, Quality PB, 978-1-58023-113-8 **$19.99**

Tears of Sorrow, Seeds of Hope, 2nd Edition: A Jewish Spiritual Companion for Infertility and Pregnancy Loss *By Rabbi Nina Beth Cardin*
6 x 9, 208 pp, Quality PB, 978-1-58023-233-3 **$18.99**

A Time to Mourn, a Time to Comfort, 2nd Edition
A Guide to Jewish Bereavement *By Dr. Ron Wolfson; Foreword by Rabbi David J. Wolpe*
7 x 9, 384 pp, Quality PB, 978-1-58023-253-1 **$21.99**

When a Grandparent Dies: A Kid's Own Remembering Workbook for Dealing with Shiva and the Year Beyond *By Nechama Liss-Levinson, PhD*
8 x 10, 48 pp, 2-color text, HC, 978-1-879045-44-6 **$15.95** *For ages 7–13*

Pastoral Care Resources
LifeLights / ™אורות החיים

LifeLights / ™אורות החיים are inspirational, informational booklets about challenges to our emotional and spiritual lives and how to deal with them. Offering help for wholeness and healing, each *LifeLight* is written from a uniquely Jewish spiritual perspective by a wise and caring soul—someone who knows the inner territory of grief, doubt, confusion and longing.

In addition to providing wise words to light a difficult path, each *LifeLight* booklet provides suggestions for additional resources for reading. Many list organizations, Jewish and secular, that can provide help, along with information on how to contact them.

Categories/Sample Topics:

Health & Healing
Caring for Yourself When You Are Caring for Someone Who Is Ill
Facing Cancer as a Family
Recognizing a Loved One's Addiction, and Providing Help

Loss / Grief / Death & Dying
Coping with the Death of a Spouse
From Death through *Shiva*: A Guide to Jewish Grieving Practices
Taking the Time You Need to Mourn Your Loss
Talking to Children about Death

Judaism / Living a Jewish Life
Bar and Bat Mitzvah's Meaning: Preparing Spiritually with Your Child
Yearning for God

Family Issues
Grandparenting Interfaith Grandchildren
Talking to Your Children about God

Spiritual Care / Personal Growth
Easing the Burden of Stress
Finding a Way to Forgive
Praying in Hard Times

Now available in hundreds of congregations, health-care facilities, funeral homes, colleges and military installations, these helpful, comforting resources can be uniquely presented in *LifeLights* display racks, available from Jewish Lights. **Each *LifeLight* topic is sold in packs of twelve for $9.95.** General discounts are available for quantity purchases.

Visit us online at **www.jewishlights.com** for a complete list of titles, authors, prices and ordering information, or call us at (802) 457-4000 or toll free at (800) 962-4544.

About Jewish Lights

People of all faiths and backgrounds yearn for books that attract, engage, educate, and spiritually inspire.

Our principal goal is to stimulate thought and help all people learn about who the Jewish People are, where they come from, and what the future can be made to hold. While people of our diverse Jewish heritage are the primary audience, our books speak to people in the Christian world as well and will broaden their understanding of Judaism and the roots of their own faith.

We bring to you authors who are at the forefront of spiritual thought and experience. While each has something different to say, they all say it in a voice that you can hear.

Our books are designed to welcome you and then to engage, stimulate, and inspire. We judge our success not only by whether or not our books are beautiful and commercially successful, but by whether or not they make a difference in your life.

For your information and convenience, at the back of this book we have provided a list of other Jewish Lights books you might find interesting and useful. They cover all the categories of your life:

Bar/Bat Mitzvah	Life Cycle
Bible Study / Midrash	Meditation
Children's Books	Men's Interest
Congregation Resources	Parenting
Current Events / History	Prayer / Ritual / Sacred Practice
Ecology / Environment	Social Justice
Fiction: Mystery, Science Fiction	Spirituality
Grief / Healing	Theology / Philosophy
Holidays / Holy Days	Travel
Inspiration	Twelve Steps
Kabbalah / Mysticism / Enneagram	Women's Interest

Stuart M. Matlins, Publisher

Or phone, fax, mail or email to: **JEWISH LIGHTS Publishing**
Sunset Farm Offices, Route 4 • P.O. Box 237 • Woodstock, Vermont 05091
Tel: (802) 457-4000 • Fax: (802) 457-4004 • www.jewishlights.com
Credit card orders: **(800) 962-4544** (8:30AM–5:30PM EST Monday–Friday)
Generous discounts on quantity orders. SATISFACTION GUARANTEED. Prices subject to change.